THE
COUNTRY
HOUSE
EXPLAINED

TREVOR YORKE

THE
COUNTRY HOUSE EXPLAINED

TREVOR YORKE

COUNTRYSIDE BOOKS
NEWBURY BERKSHIRE

First published 2003
© Trevor Yorke 2003

All rights reserved. No reproduction
permitted without the prior permission
of the publisher:

COUNTRYSIDE BOOKS
3 Catherine Road
Newbury, Berkshire

To view our complete range of books,
please visit us at
wwwcountrysidebooks.co.uk

ISBN 1 85306 793 8

Photographs and illustrations by the author
Designed by Peter Davies, Nautilus Design

Produced through MRM Associates Ltd., Reading
Printed by Woolnough Bookbinding Ltd., Irthlingborough

CONTENTS

Introduction

···⟨∞⟩···

England is blessed with a diverse landscape, a countryside of lush rolling hills, golden fields, wild moorland and rugged mountains, picturesque scenes which are further embellished by architecture. Thatched cottages, spired churches and rustic pubs are vital elements in these rural compositions, but the grandest icon, the social and economic centre of all these other components, is the country house.

The attraction of English stately homes is more than just one of architectural appreciation. They mirror the same variety of form that endears the countryside to us, with no one house being the same as the next. There are rusty coloured manor houses in the Cotswolds, stone grey fortified mansions in the northern border counties, Elizabethan red brick piles in the Midlands and black and white timber structures in Cheshire. Some are tall, imposing buildings towering over their estates, others graceful expanses of stone and glass hidden from view. They can range from humble manor houses of the local squire to palatial mansions of egotistic aristocrats.

In addition to the external structure the country house always has a deep and fascinating human story to tell. Perhaps it was the home of a great military man with trophies from his victorious battles on view, or an ancient family seat with portraits of ancestors and coats of arms proudly displayed, or sometimes it was the creation of an eccentric aristocrat whose peculiar character emerges from the mists of time in the decoration and collections encased in his fanciful abode.

To some there is more interest behind the green baize door, in the rooms occupied by those who kept the place running. There are the elaborate mechanical devices they used in the kitchen, the cool marble interiors of the dairy where they skimmed the milk and the plain wooden tables on which they ate in the servants' hall. The surrounding estate is a further attraction, with glorious terraced gardens, strange and fascinating follies and even the utilitarian farms and stable blocks adding to the appeal.

My earliest memories upon visiting one such stately home was finding, shrouded in the dark undergrowth outside, a mysterious brick tunnel with its gloomy interior barred by a gate. Was it a hidden passage leading into the house, or a chamber in which secret meetings of nobles were held, or was it part of a miniature railway line? Unfortunately for me there was no information to hand and what turned out to be an ice house was omitted from the guidebook. In later years I developed a passion for architecture and spent many hours admiring grandiose exteriors and lavish interiors. I used to find it frustrating, though, reading about a room or building when the expert called a feature by some bewildering architectural term and then set about describing its artistic merits while I was still trying to work out what I was meant to be looking at in the first place. I was sure I would get far more enjoyment from my visits if I could understand the

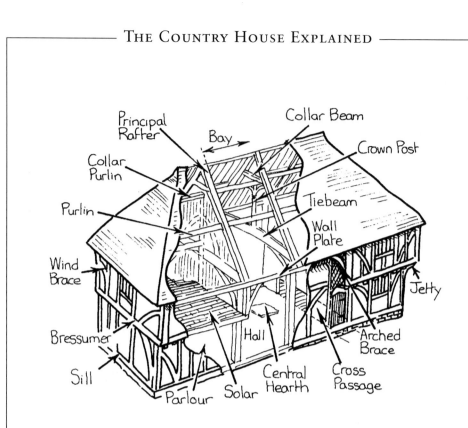

Timber frame house details

terminology, recognise the different period styles and also discover what some of these strange structures were around the estate. This book is the culmination of my search, with the relevant information passed on mainly in the form of drawings, diagrams and photographs.

The book is divided into four sections, with the first describing the various changes to the exterior of the house. This section is broken down into six chapters covering periods from the 14th century to the present day. Each one begins with a brief view of the national events and social climate that affected the aristocracy, and then is followed by

descriptions and pictures showing the style, layout and details of the houses they built. The second section travels inside, looking first at how the internal structure was designed and decorated and then describing the principal and service rooms, what they were used for and details you might find within them today. Section Three takes you on a tour of the estate, visiting the gardens, parks and even those mysterious ice houses on the way. Finally, there is a quick reference time chart listing country house architects and the notable buildings they designed, along with drawings of the period details that can help date them. There is also a glossary of those sometimes bewildering architectural terms.

I hope that after reading this book you

will enjoy an added dimension to your country house visits; that the elaborate architecture won't seem so alien, estate buildings won't appear irrelevant and the layout of the sumptuous interiors won't be so overwhelming. You will be able to recognise the Classical Orders and know that the piano nobile was not a musical instrument! You may even find that next time your companions stand awestruck in front of a towering façade of columns and pediments you can surprise them by announcing 'looks Palladian to me', and suggest they buy the teas before they have a chance to recover!

Trevor Yorke

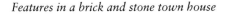

Features in a brick and stone town house

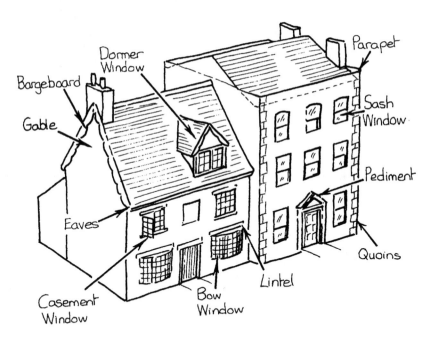

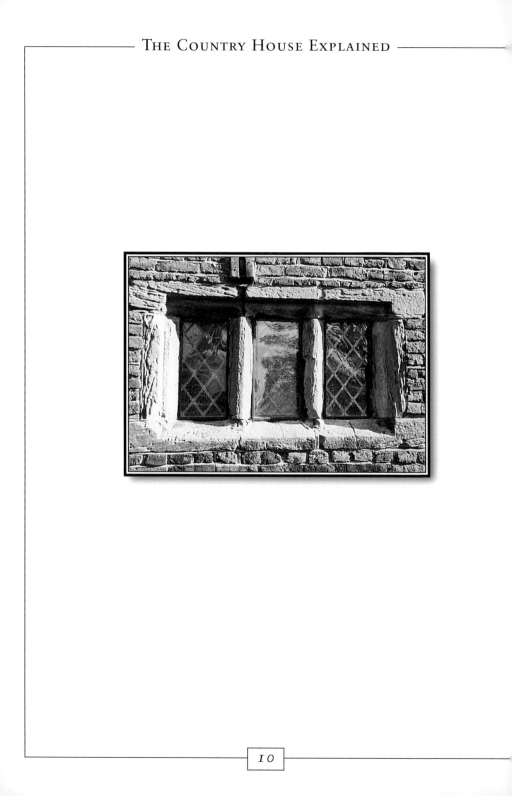

SECTION I

COUNTRY HOUSE STYLES THROUGH THE AGES

CHAPTER I

Chivalry and Gluttony

LATER MEDIEVAL AND EARLY TUDOR HOUSES
1300 - 1560

To start our journey through the history of the English country house we need to turn back the clock some 700 years to the Middle Ages. It was a time when military might and the respect it commanded were of primary importance in the life of an aspiring lord of the manor. His household officers were his show of strength, with the size of this personal army and its loyalty to him acting as a barometer of his standing among fellow nobles. He, in return, provided a roof over their heads and regarded them as an extended family.

This community would travel with their lord as he moved from one of his estates to another, a surprisingly frequent event occurring perhaps every couple of months or so and involving a huge baggage train in which even the master's bed would be included. This portable household, which encompassed a wide social spectrum from young aristocratic knights down to local peasant boys, could number into the hundreds, although many would have been based on one estate and only worked when the lord was visiting. From his house at the centre of his estate, the lord could dispense justice, organise the communal farming calendar, and hold seasonal gatherings. As these medieval country houses were derived from the castles of the 11th and 12th centuries, they still played the role of a barracks, and hence

most of the household were male, even the entire kitchen staff.

At the head of this family stood the lord, a military leader and faithful Christian, we understand, strong in his dispensation of justice yet hospitable to strangers at his door. A chivalrous and graceful socialite as much at ease with the dance or the pen as with the horse and sword. Although few would ever have attained this ideal image, these were the expectations heaped on the aspiring noble, especially from the 14th to 16th centuries. Not only therefore did he have to worry about impressing his guests with huge banquets, feasts and entertainment, but he also had to build somewhere to house them and his increasingly large household. Hence, from the earlier castles and manor houses evolves the country house.

Style of the Houses

There are a number of points in which the medieval and Early Tudor country house differs from the later buildings upon which this book concentrates. Firstly, style in itself was not a major consideration in its design, for the house was laid out with function in mind. Hence, typically in the 15th and 16th centuries, they would appear to be a jumble of buildings of various shapes and sizes usually looking in upon a courtyard with the latest in fashionable accessories, the gatehouse and chimney,

FIG 1.1: LITTLE MORETON HALL, CHESHIRE: *This rambling timber framed house has at its core a 15th century H-shaped building which in the following century was added to, with the famous gate house range on the right of the picture being the final piece of the jigsaw in the 1570s. Typically for the period the composition of the house is irregular as rules on symmetry and proportions were unknown to its builder. It also did not seem to matter that the main front, pictured here with its spectacular row of windows marking the Long Gallery at the top, had a garderobe tower (a toilet block) prominently positioned below!*

vying with each other for height.

Secondly the medieval country house was generally a vernacular building. That is, they were designed and built by a locally based mason or carpenter using local materials (the finest craftsmen and materials were employed by the two great patrons of the period, the Church and the Crown, for their cathedrals and palaces). As the local builder is unlikely

FIG 1.2: MINSTER LOVELL HALL, OXFORDSHIRE: *The photograph on the left shows the remains of the hall from this 15th century country house, with its impressive tall windows overlooking the central courtyard. The partial reconstruction on the right shows how originally it would have been somewhat lost in the midst of a range of service buildings and apartments. In the foreground of the photograph are the foundations of the kitchen, with the ring of stone on the far wall marking the well.*

to have travelled outside his region in his lifetime, he would have constructed the house using local methods passed down from generations, with the only concessions to fashion appearing in the detailing, like the shape of a window and door or the style of timber framing. The building material would have been sourced locally, so you tend to find stone in the North, West and Limestone Belt of Central England, and timber frames elsewhere. A third material, brick, makes its mark in the 15th century. The Romans had first introduced it but the manufacturing methods had been

subsequently lost until it was brought here again by the Dutch and Flemish. In this period, it was generally used in the Eastern and South Eastern areas, which had good contacts with the Low Countries.

A final difference was that military thinking influenced the layout and style of the country house, even though any defensive features would hardly ever be tested in the relatively peaceful counties away from the turbulent border regions. Moats, crenellated walls, imposing gatehouses and buildings looking inwards upon a central courtyard were all features influenced by the earlier castle and used by the owner as statements of power and wealth. Some even made their houses in the form of castles and named them thus.

Layout of the Houses

The changes in layout through the later medieval period were mainly influenced by the move away from the open communal living towards more privacy for the lord and his family. The open hall with a scattering of lesser buildings, which was typical in the 13th century, had evolved by the 16th century into a main house composed of a number of rooms with service buildings and lodgings physically attached to it. The increasing size of the household also demanded more room, with the senior servants of the lord often receiving their own private lodgings.

As there was no specific building style which would impose limitations on the layout, the way the lord expected the house to run and his preference for certain functions, which influence country houses in all periods, in this time had a free rein. So, if he wanted a large chapel which he could access from the side of his private quarters, it did not matter that it stuck out from the main hall; there were no proportions or external symmetry to worry about.

One restriction, however, may have been the site itself. For instance, the size of a moat or a defensive wall, an existing building or the lie of the land would shape the original layout and limit any latter additions. In later periods the whole house could be moved to a new, less restricted site or the existing village simply resited to suit the lord.

Exterior Details

Although the main structure was influenced by local tradition and materials, the detailing was more likely to reflect the latest trends.

In masonry structures, the doorways

FIG 1.3: TIMBER FRAMING STYLES: *Medieval framing with its distinctive large panels and curved arch braces was used in the earlier part of this period. By the 15th and 16th centuries close studding had become popular especially in the eastern counties and decorative framing in the north west. Both used excessive amounts of timber purely for decoration and were a show of the owner's wealth.*

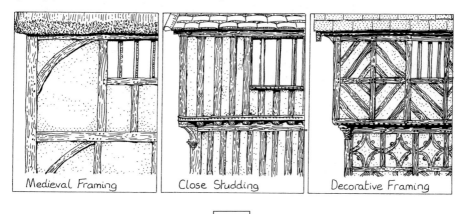

Medieval Framing   Close Studding   Decorative Framing

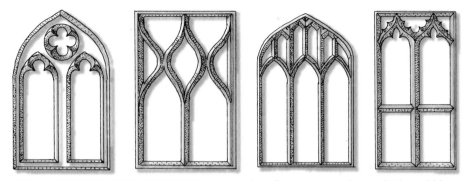

FIG 1.4: MEDIEVAL WINDOW STYLES: *Four styles of masonry windows which could be found in an important room like the hall or solar.*

and windows followed the styles of the latest church architecture. Most windows would have been square headed and of simple design, usually with one or two vertical bars (mullions), but in important rooms, especially the hall or the solar, a larger more elaborate traceried window may be found. In the 13th century the Early English style with simple lancet or plate traceried windows was usual. This evolved into the Decorated style by the early 14th century with more elaborate geometric and curvilinear shapes, being replaced in turn by the Perpendicular with its emphasis on the vertical. In timber framed houses the nature of construction means that windows had to be square or rectangular as they were just an unfilled panel between the main box-shaped frame of the house. Although they started as simple openings with a couple of mullions, by the 15th century they had developed into elaborately carved and sometimes projecting statements of wealth.

Although when you visit country houses from this period the windows are filled with glass, this was not always the

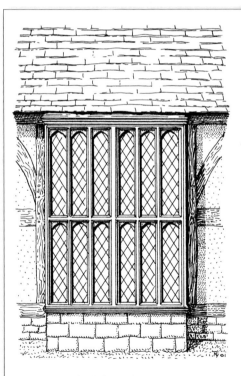

FIG 1.5: *To the left is a bay window set, in this case, in a timber framed hall,*

case when they were originally built. Many traceried windows were open to the elements with only wooden shutters, animal hide or oiled cloth curtains to keep out the draughts. Glass was a luxury item which only became common in the 15th and 16th centuries, and then mainly in the houses of the wealthy.

One place where glass, often decorated with heraldic symbols, could be used to full effect was in an oriel or a bay window. The oriel by the 16th century usually refers to a projecting window from an upper storey although earlier the word 'oriole' was applied to porches, staircases and a protrusion into an oratory (from which the word probably evolved). A bay window is one which rests on the ground and runs up more than one storey of the house, although you sometimes hear these windows referred to as an oriels in houses of this period. They were most strikingly featured at the dais end of the hall (see fig 8.2), flooding the lord with light, and also permitting those in the hall to peek out and see who was at the door.

In stone buildings, the main problem facing the mason was the distribution of weight. In early structures, the walls take the weight of the roof so windows tend to be small with round or steeply pointed

while to the right is an oriel window in a common position above a doorway.

FIG 1.6: LITTLE MORETON HALL: *Although this dates from the late 16th century it shows the style of projecting timber framed window with arrangements of small panes of glass within which was fashionable in the Tudor period. Also note that the timber frame of the house is held together by pegs which have been left slightly projecting from the wood above the window.*

arches. With improving building technology the loads were increasingly taken by clever systems of buttresses, so the walls freed from their supporting task could be pierced by larger windows with ever flatter arches. Although this technology was usually applied to cathedrals and churches, the style of windows that evolved also appeared in the houses of the wealthy. The shapes of doorways also followed this trend with the pointed arches becoming progressively flatter so by the 15th and 16th centuries they could neatly fit into a square-headed moulding. This latter style also permitted the mason to insert heraldic symbols into the top corners, and coats of arms and shields often appear above main entrances or gateways. The dramatic changes to the country house with the creation of private apartments and rooms was only possible with the introduction of the chimney (in this period, the word 'chimney' – derived from the Greek *kaminor*, oven – meant the whole

FIG 1.7: COMPTON WYNYATES, WARWICKSHIRE: *This square-headed stone doorway with circular motifs squeezed in above the arch dates from the late 15th and early 16th century.*

fireplace and stack. As these were luxury items the earliest examples are substantial stone structures often with elaborately carved openings at the top.

FIG 1.8: *The chimney below is a rare medieval example from Abingdon Abbey, Oxfordshire; the right-hand example is a more typical brick construction of the Tudor period.*

FIG 1.9

Exemplar Hall c.1400

The introduction of brick made the construction of a chimney much easier especially in the stone-free areas where the house was timber framed and, by the Tudor period, banks of excessively tall, polygonal brick stacks were a familiar sight on the skyline of the country house.

So, imagine yourself approaching Exemplar Hall (above) passing along a muddy, rutted road lined with a mix of low, timber framed cottages and a few taller, sturdy houses until you reach its imposing crenellated walls. You turn in, under the gatehouse, into a courtyard surrounded by an array of buildings with household staff busy crossing between them. The old hall is in front of you, recognisable by its large window and louvre in the roof, while behind it is the kitchen, which is separate from the main building due to its inflammable nature. To the left of the hall is a small private chapel for the use of the owner of the house. Your impression is of a scattered range of buildings with your eye drawn to the decorative incidental parts rather than the whole composition.

This typical medieval picture had developed slowly through the Middle Ages but in the 16th century things were to change with uncharacteristic speed. The new aristocracy would have different ambitions and motivations, and would use the country house as an expression of their wealth and aspirations.

CHAPTER 2

Wealth and the Humanities

·•·❰❨◊❩❩❭·•·

ELIZABETHAN AND JACOBEAN HOUSES

1560 - 1660

FIG 2.1: HARDWICK HALL, DERBYSHIRE: *Designed by Robert Smythson for Bess of Hardwick and built from 1591-97. It is radically different from medieval and earlier Tudor houses with its symmetrical façade, roof hidden behind a parapet and a greater area of glass windows than wall. This outward looking mansion was built to impress with the owner's initials crowning the dominant towers ('ES' stands for Bess's full title, Elizabeth Shrewsbury, after her fourth marriage to the Earl of Shrewsbury).*

While our aristocratic families were squabbling over the crown during the 15th century, far away in Italy a new system of education based upon the study of the Humanities (Grammar, Rhetoric, History, Poetry and Moral Philosophy) led to a fresh appreciation of Classical Greek and Roman literature, art and architecture. This rebirth is better known to us as the Renaissance (from *naissance*, the French word for birth).

The effect of the Renaissance on 16th century England was limited, mainly due to the break from Rome and Catholic Europe which resulted from Henry VIII's quest for a divorce from Catherine of Aragon. Despite this cultural isolation which lasted nearly a century, humanist teachings influenced the upper classes with the new Renaissance gentleman being expected to know Latin and Greek, have read the Scriptures and Classics, and even be able to write poetry. Men also studied the human body and the natural world, while humanist ideals made the acquisition and display of personal wealth more acceptable.

In order to keep an eye on the troublesome aristocrats who had caused their predecessors so much grief, the Tudors granted them positions of power and influence at Court. These families also increased their wealth during this period by utilising their estates better, perhaps by extracting mineral deposits or enclosing fields, while all benefited from increasing rents and food prices. By this time the ranks of the upper classes were being swelled by a new class of lesser gentry. These included courtiers, merchants and lawyers who, with a good education and by seizing opportunities, had risen to high office.

The Dissolution of the Monasteries in the late 1530s enabled Henry VIII to grant or sell their estates to courtiers and gentry. He gained political stability by positioning the right people where he wanted them, and they gained new land and houses. It was not until the relative peace and prosperity under Elizabeth I that the new owners finally knocked down the old monastic buildings or their medieval piles and erected proud, dazzling and confident houses in their place. As the Queen had built no new palaces, she relied on her subjects accommodating her on her Summer Progress, and each vied with the others to build a more sumptuous and impressive house.

The coming to the throne in 1603 of James I saw the end of hostilities with Spain and opened Europe to England once again, so that Renaissance ideas could flow more freely from the Continent. During this Jacobean age (from *Jacobus*, the Latin for James) there were exponents of Classical architecture but their influence on the country house was not to blossom until after the disruption of the Civil War and Commonwealth. In this period it is the aristocrats or gentlemen armed with an architectural pattern book from the Continent and a master mason who were the builders of country houses.

Style of the Houses

The first significant change with the new country houses of the Elizabethan Age was that they started to look outwards. Although many were still built around a courtyard, they now had a front designed to impress and one which would demonstrate to visitors the owner's good taste and wealth.

These new houses were also symmetrical. This Renaissance practice was derived from the Ancients' belief that as the Gods had made us in the image of themselves so the proportions of the human body were divine, and had symmetry. Although the English builders used some Classical motifs they did not understand the other rules of proportions and geometry which were being used by designers in Italy.

Another distinction of country houses of this period is the obsession with glass. Now that it was more readily available, the builder would seemingly use it at

FIG 2.2: MELFORD HALL, SUFFOLK: *A mid 16th century country house built by William Cordell, who became Speaker of the House of Commons. It is known to have been completed by 1578 when he entertained Queen Elizabeth I here. Towers with ogee-shaped caps, brick walls rising up to hide the roof, and the symmetrical façade were fashionable features of the time, but the hood moulding just above each window was rather outdated.*

FIG 2.3: BURGHLEY HOUSE, LINCOLNSHIRE: *Although it appears as a solid mass, this huge prodigy house built for William Cecil between the 1550s and 1580s is actually arranged around a central courtyard. Numerous windows, prominent displays of chimneys and ogee-shaped capped towers are typical Elizabethan features.*

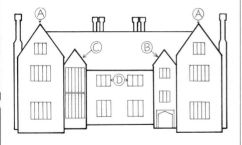

FIG 2.4: *A medieval hall with cross wings featuring pointed gables (A) at each end. The entrance to the hall was fixed at the right-hand end so, in order to update the façade for the Elizabethan fashion for symmetry, the owner has built a porch (B) to balance the bay window (C) at the other end of the hall. As chimneys with fireplaces on the back wall have replaced the old open hearth in the middle of the room, a floor has been inserted in the hall creating a Great Chamber above it (D).*

FIG 2.6: *A façade based on Longleat House, Wiltshire, which was the nearest 16th century England got to a Renaissance house. The Classically-styled front is a mass of glass with a parapet hiding the roof (I) and a horizontal moulding called an entablature (J) running around the house at each floor level.*

FIG 2.5: *When the owner built the house from scratch he could site the entrance porch (E) in the middle, with the hall in this case to the left (F) and the service rooms to the right (G). Another benefit of inserting floors now the old central hearth had gone, was that a third attic floor could be built, usually for servants' lodgings (H).*

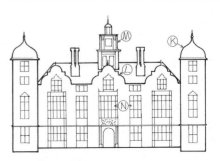

FIG 2.7: *An early 17th century façade based on Blickling Hall, Norfolk. Towers with ogee-shaped caps (K), Dutch gables (L) and on the roof a cupola (M) were all popular features. The tallest windows (N) mark the most important floor in a country house, usually the state apartments. Previously these would have been on the ground floor, but increasingly they were raised.*

every opportunity. The solid mass of medieval walls was replaced by shimmering façades of oversized windows. The walls themselves were now of stone or brick, the latter often decorated with diamond patterns in a different colour (diaper patterns). Another distinct feature of Elizabethan and Jacobean walls was the use of a continuous entablature, a horizontal decorative trim which ran all around the house at the various floor levels. It helped to hold together visually the sometimes bewildering sets of towers and bays.

The most familiar style of the more modest country house in the late 16th and early 17th centuries was the E-shaped plan, with its symmetrical façade and pointed gables to the front (figs 2.4 and 2.5).

PRODIGY HOUSES

There was no one dominant style in this period and no true architects to build in

FIG 2.8: WOLLATON HALL, NOTTINGHAM: *This impressive prodigy house was designed by Robert Smythson and has many similar characteristics to Hardwick and Longleat with which he was also involved. The raised central section with its round corner turrets stands above the hall and gives the whole mass the air of a castle.*

it. The most famous designer of the Elizabethan country house was Robert Smythson who constructed magnificent towers and bays of glass at Hardwick Hall in Derbyshire and Wollaton Hall, now within Nottingham. These and the other huge country houses which were erected with a visit from the Monarch in mind have been christened 'prodigy houses'. Hatfield House in Hertfordshire and Audley End in Essex are examples which were built after James I came to the throne.

⊞ ARTISAN MANNERISM

Contacts with our Protestant allies in the Low Countries had already seen the import of details like Dutch gables (figs 2.7 and 2.9), but now as the restrictions on travel to the Continent were receding, Renaissance ideas flowed more freely. By this stage, the architects in Europe had long become bored by the limitations of the strict Classical rules and had started bending them. This more playful style labelled as Artisan Mannerism in England started to bear fruit in the reign of Charles I, only for the Civil War to halt its progress.

The first great English architect worked during this Jacobean period but despite his ground-breaking understanding of the principles of Classical architecture the limited purse strings of the monarchy meant few of his plans ever made it past the drawing board. Inigo Jones's genius would have to wait a hundred years before influencing our country houses.

FIG 2.9: HATFIELD HOUSE, HERTFORDSHIRE: *There is a distinct Renaissance feel to the central section of the south front of this Jacobean house. The arched openings along the ground floor (known as a loggia), the Classical columns and pilasters, and the Dutch gables are all features copied from houses of the period on the Continent. The twin pairs of columns on the central porch are typical of the late 16th and early 17th century.*

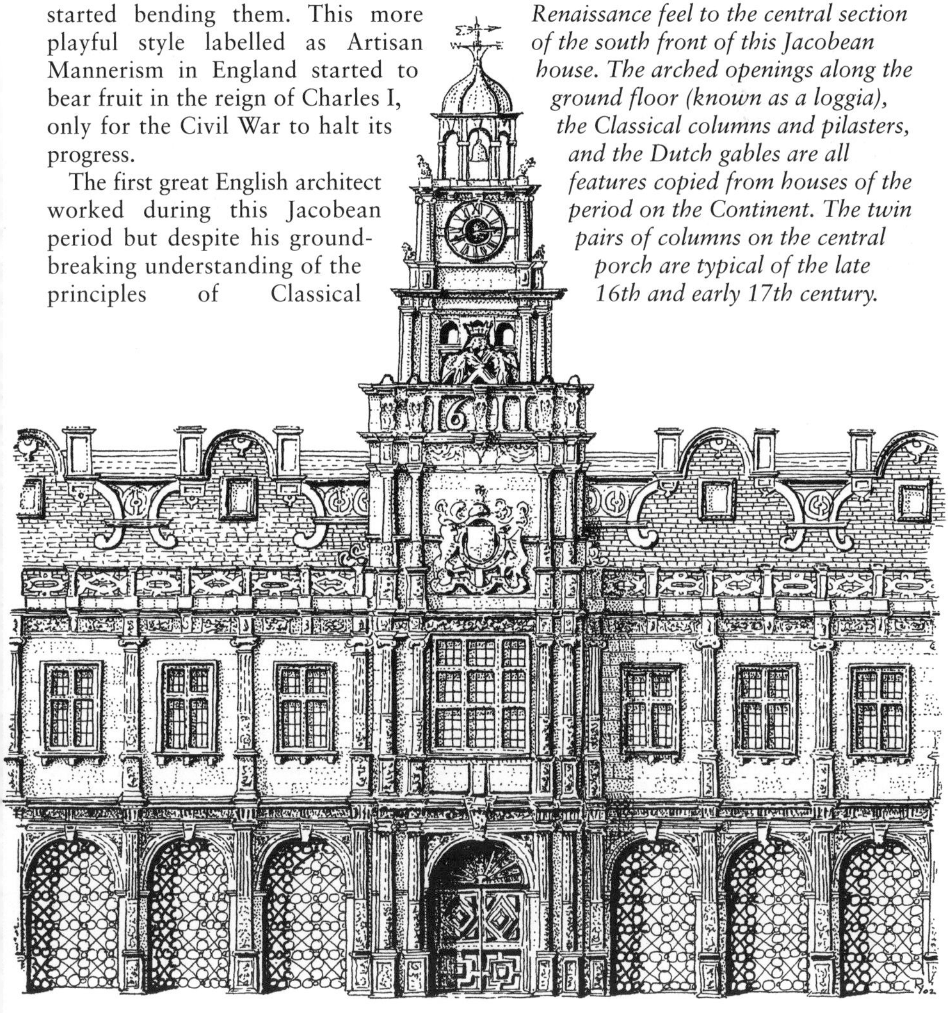

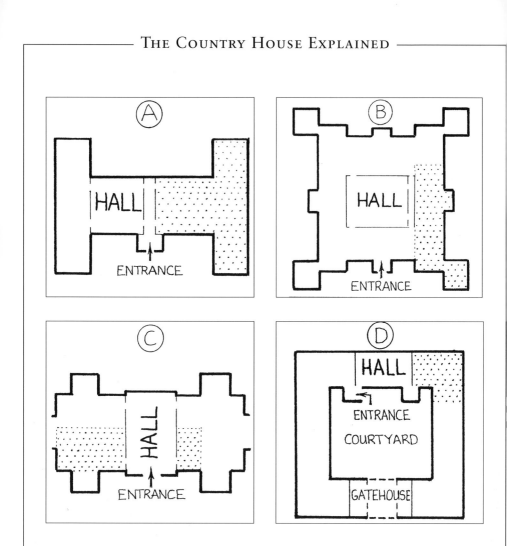

FIG 2.10: *Four simplified plans of country houses of this period showing the all-important position of the hall. The stippled areas are the service rooms including the kitchen. (A) shows the layout of the house in fig 2.5, with the hall now offset so the porch is in the middle of the front and the kitchen and food storage rooms are the other side of the central passage. (B) is a plan of Wollaton Hall (fig 2.8) which, despite its Classical pretensions, still has the hall in its medieval position with the entrance from a passage on the right-hand end. (C) is Hardwick Hall where the room has now been turned around 90° so that the entrance is still conveniently at the end of the hall but the symmetry of the front is maintained. (D) shows another popular layout which gave the approaching guests the impression of a massive house but was only four blocks of one room depth around a central courtyard. The hall is still in its traditional position with a porch and bay window at each end.*

Layout of the Houses

The well-educated Elizabethan revelled in a secret language of symbols and hidden meanings which even extended to the plan of the house. The E-shaped plan could have implied homage to the Queen or to Emmanuel, while the designer John Thorpe even planned a house in the shape of his own initials. Geometric shapes, especially circles, triangles and crosses could form the basis of the layout, for instance the Triangular Lodge at Rushton in Northamptonshire represented the Trinity and symbolised the owner's Catholic faith.

The change of role of the country house from the communal centre of a

---

FIG 2.11: *A cut out view of an imaginary modest country house of this period, showing a popular arrangement with the hall on the opposite side of the entrance from the service rooms. The long gallery runs along one of the wings though it could also be found along the length of the house, on the second or third floors.*

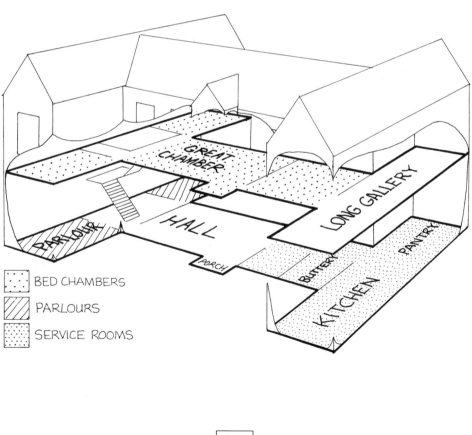

BED CHAMBERS

PARLOURS

SERVICE ROOMS

manor to the private residence of a cultured noble can be seen in the layout of Elizabethan and Jacobean houses. In earlier houses the hall dominated the main part of the house but as it was entered from one end the main entrance was sited off centre. As the appreciation of symmetry grew and the hall fell from importance, the room could be resited and a central porch positioned in the middle of the façade (see fig 2.5). At Hardwick, the hall was for the first time turned round end on to the front making symmetry easier, and thus the hall became the entrance room with which we associate it today.

With this move to privacy, an ever increasing assemblage of rooms evolved. They could now be spread over three rather than two floors although the depth of the house was still usually one room thick. In larger houses there might be a series of state apartments on an upper floor for entertaining and impressing important and preferably royal guests. These are usually discernible from the exterior by the row of highest windows. There would then be further private apartments for the family while the staff still ate in the hall, but then as this became an entrance area in the 17th century a separate servants' hall was provided.

The kitchen had now moved inside the building, thanks to stone and brick fireplaces set within the wall instead of open hearths for cooking – which greatly reduced the fire risk. A fashionable accessory to any aspiring lord's house, which is almost exclusive to this period, is the long gallery. This was a thin rectangular room which usually spanned the entire length or width of the main room with a bank of windows on one or occasionally both sides (see page 121).

Exterior Details

FIG 2.12: *A typical 16th and early 17th century window from a country house. The windows were almost exclusively square or rectangular masonry frames with a number of fixed horizontal bars (transoms) and vertical bars (mullions). As there was not the technology yet to make large pieces of glass, the windows were filled with small panes held in place by lead strips in a square or diamond pattern.*

FIG 2.13: *A smaller window with just a couple of mullions. This would typically be found on the top attic floor, in the earliest houses with basements and in outbuildings like this example from a mill at Dunham Massey in Cheshire.*

FIG 2.14: *The chimneys in this period tended to have individual stacks for each fireplace below them joined at the top, and were often found in rows like this example. Brick and stone were used for their construction, although there were also some ingenious designs like at Wollaton Hall (fig 2.20) where the chimneys were disguised behind the parapet of the tower.*

FIG 2.15: LYME PARK, CHESHIRE: *The humble entrance to the medieval house was superseded in this period by flamboyant, if sometimes clumsy porches. They are discernible by their height and narrowness, and by the stacked series of Classical ornaments and columns with a small round-headed doorway below. Even on a brick house they are usually made of stone. This example on the north front of Lyme Hall incorporates all these features although the top section with the statue was added at a later date.*

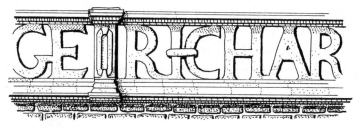

FIG 2.17: *Brickwork with a 'diaper' pattern made from darker bricks which were vitrified by over burning or the addition of salt in the firing stage of their construction. Bricks of this period were hand made either on the site or at local brickworks. They were usually thinner and longer than modern machine -made examples, and tended to be about 9 x 2½ inches in size. The pattern formed by the differing arrangements of bricks is known as bonding and it varies through the ages. In the 16th century English bond, which was formed from alternate layers with the small end of a brick (headers) showing followed by a row with the long side (stretchers) exposed, was popular.*

FIG 2.16: BLICKLING HALL, NORFOLK: *This corner tower is a common feature of 16th and early 17th century houses. Of brick construction with stone corner blocks (quoins) in a tooth effect it is finished off with a cap in a distinctive 'S' profile, a shape known as ogee, and also found in arches and doorways from the period.*

FIG 2.18: *The parapet along the top of walls hid the roof from view and gave the building a more imposing, Classical form. In this period many were punctuated with initials (as in the top of the towers at Hardwick in fig 2.1) or, as in this case, actual words made out of stone.*

FIG 2.19: *This pattern of swirls and straights formed by flat pieces of masonry slightly raised above the surrounding stone wall, is known as 'strapwork'. It is a very distinctive feature of Elizabethan and Jacobean houses and although it can be found in various places including ceilings, it is most commonly seen decorating the tops of towers, gables and parapets.*

FIG 2.21: BURGHLEY HOUSE, NORTHAMPTONSHIRE: *A close up of the chimneys, linked at the top, and the parapet with pinnacles which mark out the roof line. The large pyramid obelisk stands above an entrance into the inner courtyard.*

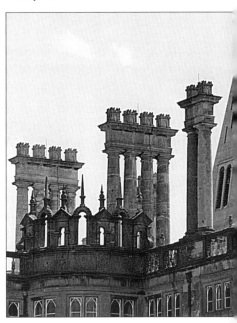

FIG 2.20: WOLLATON HALL, NOTTINGHAM: *A tower which includes a medley of popular Elizabethan features including strapwork and pinnacles on the top, large windows flanked by pilasters (flat columns built into the wall), and continuous entablatures wrapping horizontally around the tower on each floor level. Note the four visible chimneys at the very top ingeniously disguised as part of the masonry behind the decorative crest at the top of the tower.*

FIG 2.22

Exemplar Hall c.1600

Two hundred years have passed since we last visited Exemplar Hall and the recent lords of the manor have made modest progress and have embellished their family home rather than rebuilding it. The entrance is marked by an impressive brick gatehouse with the courtyard beyond now lined with new lodgings and service buildings. A small concession to symmetry appears on the front of the main hall which has a large bay window to the left and a tall porch balancing it to the right. A new kitchen has been built on the right side of the house and the area at the rear where it previously stood has now become a garden.

English country houses like this were still amateur attempts at architecture, a sometimes clumsy mix of traditional English forms with the latest in foreign Classical decoration. Now a new breed of aristocrat and artisan, better acquainted with the theory and styles of European architecture, began to design new forms of houses which were emulated at all levels of the upper classes from the monarchy down to the lesser gentry.

CHAPTER 3

Commerce and Science

RESTORATION AND WILLIAM AND MARY HOUSES
1660 - 1720

Religious and constitutional differences erupted into Civil War in 1642, and after the subsequent Parliamentary victory a large number of aristocrats and gentry lay dead or fled abroad to France and the Low Countries. They returned from exile when the monarchy was restored

---

FIG 3.1: BELTON HOUSE, LINCOLNSHIRE: *This late 17th century house is a slightly shrunken copy of Clarendon House by Roger Pratt, which along with Coleshill in Berkshire influenced the design of numerous country houses in this period. Note the swagged motif and two oval windows within the triangular pediment above the doorway, which are Baroque details becoming fashionable at the time. Belton was built rapidly between 1684 and 1687 but has stood virtually unaltered for three hundred years unlike its forerunner Clarendon House which only lasted 17 years, being demolished the year before Belton was started.*

FIG 3.2: SUDBURY HALL, DERBYSHIRE: *A house primarily of the 1660s and 1670s which looks backwards as much as forwards. Despite the fashionable features on this south front like the cupola, parapet, dormer windows and plain rectangular chimneys, it has by this period outdated details like diaper diamond patterned brickwork and Jacobean style mullioned windows. This may be due to the tastes of the owner, George Vernon, who like many at the time still acted as his own architect.*

in 1660 and Charles II took the throne. The population welcomed him, but Parliament was more cautious and limited his powers and purse strings, hence he relied on the French King, Louis XIV, for financial support.

In a period of religious tensions with the Puritans at one end of the spectrum and the Papists (Roman Catholics) at the other, the King trod a careful diplomatic line, only revealing his true faith on his deathbed. Although Charles had kept his Catholic leanings secret, his brother James who succeeded him in 1685 did not, yet despite Anglican England's fanatical fear of papal influence the new King was generally accepted especially as his daughters were Protestant and his new Catholic wife seemed unlikely to provide him with a male heir. Unfortunately for James that was exactly what happened and with the birth of this Catholic son and the trial of Anglican bishops, a group of lords invited the Protestant William of Orange, who was married to Charles II's daughter Mary, to invade and claim the throne.

The subsequent constitutional changes known as the Glorious Revolution increased Parliamentary powers and gave the aristocracy supremacy over the monarch, a situation which was to last up to the end of the 19th century. As a result they gained the opportunity to increase their wealth especially with perks from their new positions of office. This was also the period of commercial revolution and many aristocrats grew rich on foreign enterprise.

There had been a drift towards the cities from the early 17th century, and many of the upper classes locked up their country properties over winter and lived in new town houses, especially in London. Towards the close of the century, though, there was a move in the opposite direction as the aristocracy chose to live on their country estates rather than just visit, giving them the opportunity to rent out their urban properties and further increase their wealth.

Science blossomed in this period, heightened by a desire to understand and control nature in the face of what many believed was the impending End of the World! The gulf widened further between the cultured gentleman with this new scientific learning and his illiterate household staff still influenced by medieval superstitions. The building of the house within which they all resided was still likely to be the project of the owner, but now he was aided by an architect, not necessarily a full time professional but an educated gentleman who had studied the fashionable building styles on the Continent and

FIG 3.3: HAM HOUSE, SURREY: *The south (garden) front of what was originally a Jacobean H-shaped house by the banks of the Thames near Richmond. In the later 17th century the Lauderdales filled in the gap between the two prongs of the H with a new range of rooms featuring early examples of sash windows, with oval-shaped ones along the bottom (the angled bay windows towards each end were restyled later).*

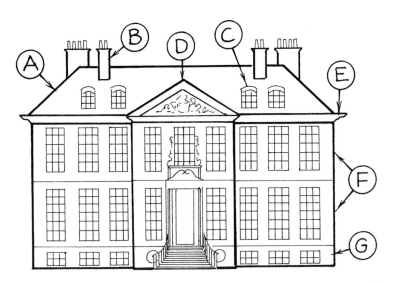

FIG 3.4: *A Dutch style façade based on Uppark, Sussex. On top is the hipped roof (A), with rectangular chimneys (B), and dormer windows (C); a pediment (D) and a deep cornice (E) are below. There are two rows of tall windows (F); those in the lower row are slightly longer indicating that this floor contains the principal rooms. The half height windows below (G) illuminate the basement.*

grasped the principles of Classical architecture. They were rarely educated in this art; John Vanbrugh for instance had been a Captain in the Marines while Christopher Wren practised anatomy, yet these men of ingenuity replaced the masons and carpenters as the builders of country houses.

Style of the Houses

The period after the Civil War up until the early 1700s was dominated by two distinct styles of country house. Both are Classical in origin although some medievalism can still be found in their planning. They therefore owe their design to foreign influences; few would contemplate building their mansions and manor houses in a vernacular style any more.

▨ DUTCH STYLE

The first style evolved from the work, what little there was, of Inigo Jones and from the Dutch Palladian style of houses which was seen by those exiled in Holland. The most influential house in this country was Coleshill in Berkshire, built in the early 1650s by Sir Roger Pratt (but now demolished). It established a style of a plain façade with two rows of tall but roughly equal sized windows topped by a deep overhanging cornice. Above this was a prominent hipped roof broken up by lines of dormer windows, stout rectangular chimneys, and crowned by a palisaded walkway and cupola. Stone and especially brick with stone quoins (a column of raised stones marking the

FIG 3.5: BLENHEIM PALACE, OXFORDSHIRE: *The north façade of the central part of this monumental palace was designed primarily by John Vanbrugh and paid for by the Crown as a reward for the Duke of Marlborough's victories over the French. Note the array of different sized windows, some with round heads, others with the arch stretched to make an oval-shaped top. The arrangement of columns supporting a triangular pediment over the entrance is called a portico, while the raised section behind this is the upper part of the great hall which harks back to Wollaton Hall (see fig 2.8). Vanbrugh not only used the latest Baroque fashions but blended them with Ancient Rome and a bit of medieval England.*

corner of the house) were popular for the walls. This simple yet impressive building type mixed in with some of the latest in Dutch fashion, and usually with a pediment added to emphasise the main entrance, formed the basis for the homes of especially the lesser gentry for the next fifty years (see fig 3.1).

These distinctive late 17th century houses are among the easiest to recognise at a glance with any variation coming in their plan and layout rather than their façade.

⬛ BAROQUE

Many architectural styles have their name coined by the next generation of designers as an insult to what they regard as an outdated or inappropriate fashion. In this case later critics labelled the buildings of the late 17th and early 18th century with their fanciful shapes, opulent decoration and irregular skyline 'Baroque', derived from a word meaning a misshaped pearl!

Baroque has its origins in the 16th

century reforms of the Catholic Church which were a reaction to the Protestant threat. A new form of art evolved which was designed to stupefy and impress upon the viewer the everlasting and unchanging nature of Heaven. A good example of this can be seen in the change of fashion in portraits. Think of a picture of an Elizabethan gentleman, in which he is standing upright with his hand on hip. All is stationary and two dimensional. Now think of the well-known Van Dyke portrait of Charles I on his bucking horse. Produced only a few decades later yet full of movement and drama, it is a three dimensional view with sweeping vistas and angels flying around with rather effeminate ribbons! This change would also be mirrored in architecture.

As the lesser gentry were turning to the Dutch prototypes for their new homes upon return from exile, the wealthier aristocrats looked to France for inspiration. The English Baroque style which evolved did not take shape until the first decades of the 1700s with the building of palatial houses like Castle Howard in Yorkshire and Blenheim Palace in Oxfordshire, as their owners waited for political stability before investing their fortunes in stone. These are characterised by their monumental scale, façades which step or curve in and out, and a skyline of pinnacles and towers which owes as much to the medieval castle as to Continental sources.

Other houses of this brief English Baroque period may have been, like Chatsworth, a piecemeal reconstruction or just a refacing of an existing building, which in either case limited the shape of the structure, so it is in the detailing of the façade that the style shines through. As many of the new houses at the time were still of a rectangular plan with a flat front, it is the architect's playful distortion of the Classical elements, the varying shapes and arrangements of windows and dramatic decoration which identify the building as Baroque. Oval-shaped features replace the geometric

---

FIG 3.6: *A Baroque façade based on Castle Howard showing the main body of the building which contained the principal rooms, flanked by two separate wings. The kitchen courtyard (H) contained the service rooms while the stable courtyard (I) which John Vanbrugh designed was never built, but a larger wing of a different style was erected some thirty years later. Note how the domes (J), the variation in height, and the statues and vases mounted along the parapet (K) make a dramatic skyline to the house.*

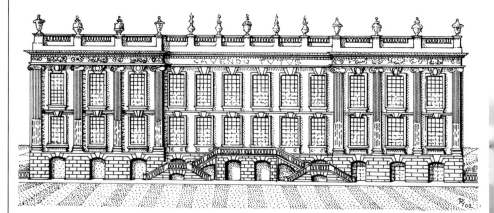

FIG 3.7: CHATSWORTH HOUSE, DERBYSHIRE: *This house was originally an Elizabethan structure built by Bess of Hardwick's husband. The architect William Talman was invited to design new Baroque-styled south and east fronts for the 1st Duke of Devonshire in 1687. However, the architect was limited by the existing structure. so that the principal rooms are on the top rather than the ground floor as was becoming fashionable at this time, and an even number of windows across the façade rather than the usual odd number which would permit a central feature.*

patterns of previous houses, and flamboyant ornaments litter the façades which in the next period would be plain.

Layout of the Houses

The major change in the planning of country houses after the Restoration was a layout with two rows of rooms one behind the other, called 'double pile'. Previously most houses were of a single room thickness and were laid out around a courtyard or with wings which gave the impression of mass when viewed from the outside. This made roofing the house easy, but now with two rooms to cover the necessary pitch would have made the roof ridiculously tall. So on these Dutch style houses the roof appears chopped off and a parapeted walkway was run around the perimeter with a cupola mounted in the middle (see fig 3.8). The roof was actually made from two separate pitches with the gap between them levelled over, though on many it was left open.

Another significant change was that, although they had been used before, it became almost universal to have a basement. The advantages of this were, firstly, as the social gulf between the lord and his staff had now widened, it was convenient to place the engine room of the house out of sight, along with its smells and noise. Secondly, as there would have to be some light in the basement, it was not built completely below ground so that a row of low windows could be inserted. This in turn meant that the ground floor of the house was raised which had the desirable effect of making the entrance, now up a row of exterior steps, more impressive to the visitor and helped reduced the problem of damp.

At the top of the house it was now the norm to have an attic floor. In these Dutch style houses with their massive sloping roofs it meant that a row of small wedged-shaped windows, called dormers, sticking out of the tiles, was the only way of lighting these rooms. With accommodation now spread over four floors the actual ground plan of the house could become more compact. A stone or brick vaulted ceiling could also be used above the basement, which was valuable protection against fire, the greatest risk of which came from the kitchen below.

The arrangement of the rooms also changes through the 17th century. Houses like Coleshill still had the state apartments on the first floor and they would be approached up an ever more elaborate staircase, sometimes rising out of the hall itself, relegating it to its present role of a reception room. Thus a visitor would climb the outside steps to

---

FIG 3.8: *A cut out view of an imaginary mid 17th century house which still has the state apartments on the first floor, the family rooms on the ground and the service rooms in the basement.*

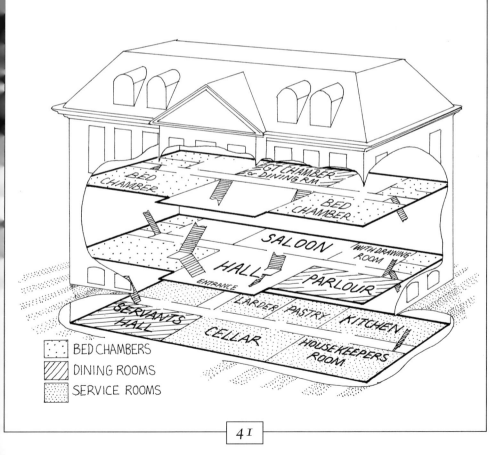

BED CHAMBERS

DINING ROOMS

SERVICE ROOMS

the now raised ground floor then ascend the interior staircase until finally reaching the principal first floor (the floor with the state apartments is referred to as the principal floor or piano nobile). Unlike earlier and later houses the height of the windows was roughly the same on ground and first floors rather than raised to emphasise the principal floor.

Access to the rooms from the main or secondary staircases would be via corridors; a spinal one which ran the full length of the house, between the front and back rooms, was common. The interiors of the country house were no longer rabbit warrens where rooms were entered via other rooms or narrow winding corridors. Now the same disciplines of symmetry and proportion which were applied to the exterior started to influence the layout of rooms within.

FIG 3.9: CHATSWORTH HOUSE, DERBYSHIRE: *The classic view of the west front of Chatsworth House. By the time the 1st Duke of Devonshire came to rebuild this façade he had fallen out with Talman (see fig 3.7) and this front was probably the work of Thomas Archer. As there are an odd number of windows a central pedimented feature could be used with the coat of arms set in the tympanum.*

In the later Baroque houses it became usual to have the state apartments on the ground floor, thus the grand staircase in the hall was no longer required. Instead the guests walked directly through to the saloon behind and from here could turn left or right to access the luxurious withdrawing rooms and bedchambers. It became fashionable to have these rooms laid out one after the other along the rear

FIG 3.10: *A plan (based on Blenheim Palace) showing the arrangement of rooms across the rear of the main building so that all the doors line up to form the enfilade. Note that in this Baroque house the state apartments or principal rooms are on the ground floor so that a huge staircase in the hall is no longer required and discreetly positioned stairs lead up to the family's private rooms.*

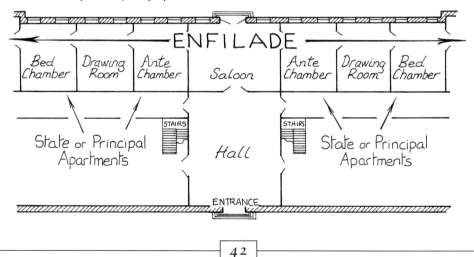

of the house with the doorways in line with each other. This is known as the enfilade. In a period of processions and ceremonies the length of this enfilade became something of a status symbol.

The larger Baroque houses further emphasised their monumental scale by having separate courtyards to the side of the central house or flanking the entrance area. One would usually contain the service rooms like the kitchen, access from which to the dining room would be via corridors or even the open air, which helped reduce the fire risk and the odours and noise. The other courtyard could contain the stables and coach houses.

Exterior Details

FIG 3.12: BLENHEIM PALACE, OXFORDSHIRE: *A monumental sized Baroque doorway showing – typically of the style – an arched top with the feature above broken by the keystone of the arch. The horizontal grooves cut into the side pillars are known as channelled rustication, and were a favourite decoration of the architect John Vanbrugh.*

FIG 3.11: SUTTON SCARSDALE HALL, DERBYSHIRE: *Although this is a Baroque house this doorway is typical of the mid to late 17th century house, square headed with a pediment above. One shaped like this is known as a segmented pediment though they could equally be triangular.*

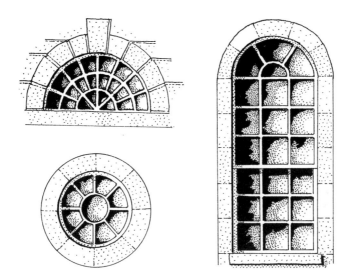

FIG 3.13: *A selection of arched and round windows from Baroque houses.*

FIG 3.14: HAM HOUSE, SURREY: *In the late 17th century sash windows appeared for the first time on country houses. It is hazardous to try and date a house from the style of window as they were frequently changed at a later date, but in general the older sash windows have thicker glazing bars and frames, the latter being often flush with the surrounding wall.*

FIG 3.16: SUDBURY HALL, DERBYSHIRE: *Gone were the twisted and decorated tall chimneys of the previous century, now they were stout rectangular blocks in brick or stone, often with a cornice around the top matching that which ran around the house below.*

FIG 3.15: SUTTON SCARSDALE HALL, DERBYSHIRE: *A close up of a window frame with the Baroque swirls decorated with flowers and fruit. This style of carving was also a very popular form of interior decoration in the late 17th and early 18th century.*

FIG 3.17: SUTTON SCARSDALE HALL, DERBYSHIRE: *In later Baroque houses parapets were reintroduced around the top of the house to help hide the chimneys so they would not spoil the Classic skyline of domes and statues.*

FIG 3.18: UPPARK, SUSSEX: *A common feature on Dutch style houses was a deep overhanging cornice with, as in this case, elegantly carved brackets and moulding. It was also popular to have light coloured stone quoins finishing off the end of the brick façade.*

FIG 3.19: SUDBURY HALL, DERBYSHIRE: *A stone cupola mounted as a central feature on the roof and granting the owner and his guests views over his surrounding parkland. Unfortunately many cupolas or domes were later removed along with the balustrades which lined the top of the roof, when a house was restyled.*

FIG 3.20: BLENHEIM PALACE, OXFORDSHIRE: *A selection of Baroque features decorate this entrance to the kitchen courtyard. Note the banded columns each side of the doorway, the mix of arched and square-headed windows and in the top left corner part of one of the peculiar towers emblazoned with all manner of arches, brackets and finials.*

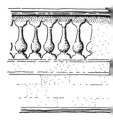

FIG 3.22: SUTTON SCARSDALE HALL, DERBYSHIRE: *The triangular pediment supported by Corinthian columns which stands above the entrance to the east front. The panel within it is known as the tympanum and it was often usual in this period for it to be decorated with a coat of arms.*

FIG 3.21: CHATSWORTH HOUSE, DERBYSHIRE: *A section of parapet which crowned the top of this Baroque house and helped to hide the roof and chimneys. The vases which stand on top, which could equally have been statues, gave the house a distinctive skyline.*

FIG 3.23: SUTTON SCARSDALE HALL: *The east front also features giant pilasters, the flat columns which run up the full height of the building, and horizontal channels in the masonry (rustication) which are both distinctive Baroque country house features. The top window with its raised frame, side scrolls and central keystone above is also typical of this date.*

Many things have changed since we last looked down on Exemplar Hall, one hundred years ago. The rambling collection of medieval and Tudor buildings has been swept aside to make way for a new Dutch style house financed by the current lord of the manor's foreign investments. The old chapel which is just to the left of the main building is the only part retained, while the parish church on the other side of the wall is looking neglected. To the right the site has expanded out into what were previously fields and a new stable courtyard with an arched entrance has been erected.

Behind the house the garden has been terraced and the main estate farm (Home Farm) has been masked off by trees and landscaping. In the bottom left of the picture some of the old cottages have been removed to achieve a better view of the lord's parkland from the front of the house. The separation between manor house and village is growing with only a few larger farms remaining.

To the older villagers this exclusion from the lord's daily life would have been viewed with regret and the shocking modernity of his new country house must have provided a visual emphasis of this great leap forward. Yet within a generation this flamboyant style of building would seem outdated and inappropriate and would in turn be replaced by new, strict forms of Classicism and radical changes to the very landscape around them.

FIG 3.24

CHAPTER 4

Liberty and Sensibility

GEORGIAN HOUSES
1720 - 1800

FIG 4.1: LYME PARK, CHESHIRE: *As with many country houses, this was originally a Tudor mansion (see fig 2.15) which the Legh family in the 1720s asked the Venetian architect Giacomo Leoni to update in the latest Classical style. This view shows the dramatic south front with many of the typical Palladian features like the rusticated masonry along the lower section, the tall windows on the first floor illuminating the piano nobile, and the portico in the centre capped off by a plain triangular pediment. There are still a few touches here though, like the flat pilasters running up the wall and the vases on top of the portico, which could have been found on Baroque houses.*

Those who had supported the exclusion of James II from the crown and had welcomed the subsequent Glorious Revolution in 1688 had risen in power and in 1715 after the accession to the throne of George I they removed great swathes of the old landed gentry from high office. These Whigs (from *Whiggamore*, a term for Scottish Covenanters who had also opposed James II) were to dominate the developing political map during the 18th century, excluding the Tories (from *toriadhe*, which was Irish for an outlaw, an insult aimed at supporters of James II) from office until the accession of George III. It was these aristocrats in high office, rather than the reclusive Hanoverian monarchs, who were the cultural leaders of their day.

The Whigs under Robert Walpole, the first so called Prime Minister, claimed to be champions of commerce and investment, fighting for Liberty as opposed to tyrannical rule. They imagined themselves as senators in Imperial Rome complete with toga and olive crown rather than just country gentlemen. Where else would they therefore want to send their sons other than to Italy? Helped by a more relaxed attitude to religious differences, the young aristocrats were sent off on Grand Tours into the heart of Catholic Europe to see the Art and Architecture primarily of Ancient Rome and the Renaissance.

The 18th century aristocrat gradually developed from a collector of curiosities into an art connoisseur. He would amass books and prints rather than displays of arms, would belong to societies devoted perhaps to Ancient Architecture or Archaeology, and he could open his mind to emotions and appreciate the beauty and drama in nature. In other words it became acceptable to be a bit of a sensitive chap! This lifestyle did not come cheap, and these gentlemen would benefit from some knowledge of developments in science, industry and agriculture to increase their incomes, especially in relation to their country

estates which for many were their main financial source. Improvement was the order of the day and enclosure of the fields on their land was one of the most controversial and still visible marks that it made.

In the second half of the 18th century Britain was doing rather well internationally; London became the chief financial centre and the defeat of France in 1763 brought about many commercial gains. Aristocratic sons adventured on the High Seas, took up posts abroad or developed trading companies, returning with great wealth to enhance their family estates. The Industrial Revolution was also under way, and there was money to be made in the new factories, quarries and mines.

FIG 4.2: CHISWICK HOUSE, LONDON: *This startling villa was designed by the 3rd Earl of Burlington from 1723-29. He promoted the architecture of Palladio and its later interpretation by Inigo Jones and statues of the two men stand at the base of the stairs (just out of view). The plan of the house is square with a symmetrical layout of rooms, good to look at but the lack of flexibility in the size and position of living areas made it an impractical design.*

These increasingly wealthy Britons sought to find a true British identity and started to look within their own shores rather than in the Ancient World. They found their beloved Liberty in the Magna Carta, the barons defending their rights against the tyrannical King John, and it became accepted that our cultural strength lay in the fact that we were composed of many different ethnic groups.

This period of rapid development was halted by the French Revolution and the subsequent war with Napoleon from 1793 onwards. Aristocratic families and the ruling classes felt for the first time insecure and suddenly Liberty and Sensibility with their French associations seemed inappropriate.

Style of the Houses

This period is dominated by Classical architecture. Few houses were built in any other style until the last decades of the century, and the Ancients' rules of proportion and architectural orders filtered down to even the most humble terraced houses. To the refined Georgian aristocrat, good taste was of primary importance, and his country house would reflect this in its reserved and strict adherence to these Classical rules and Orders. Only later in the period would it become acceptable again to bend the rules as Baroque architects had previously done.

▦ PALLADIAN

In the opening years of the reign of George I a dramatically new style of house started to appear across the country, one which was principally used by and has since been associated with the new Whig aristocrats. This style was championed by two men, Colen Campbell and Lord Burlington, who were determined to remove the flamboyant excesses of the Baroque influence and return to pure Classical architecture as determined by the Roman Vitruvius and the later Renaissance architects.

FIG 4.3: NOSTELL PRIORY, WEST YORKSHIRE: *This Palladian house begun in 1733 was never completed as originally planned with separate pavilions (see fig 4.9). Robert Adam was employed after 1765 and he built the north wing with the portico – to the right of the main house in this picture.*

We had never really embraced the Renaissance in this country, principally due to the religious break with Rome in the 1530s, just as it was starting to filter onto our shores. The architectural books written by its proponents in Italy were used to shape the detailing rather than the structure of English houses. The first architect here to grasp the Classical rules was Inigo Jones but those who followed him had turned to Dutch and French prototypes for their inspiration, forms which in the early decades of the 18th century started to seem corrupt and debased. Through Campbell and Burlington the drawings and work of Jones was rediscovered and became influential. At the same time a book of plans of one of the Renaissance architects who had inspired Jones was republished, and it was his interpretation of Ancient Roman buildings which was to dominate the designs of these new houses. His name was Andrea Palladio and hence this style is known as Palladianism.

The first influential building in this new style was Wanstead House, London (demolished in 1824) by Colen Campbell. It introduced the characteristic Palladian façade with a rusticated masonry base below the first floor or piano nobile which housed the state apartments. This floor was

FIG 4.4: Two Palladian façades. *The first one, based on Holkham Hall in Norfolk, shows how, rather than the Baroque habit of massing blocks and curves up to a crescendo in the middle, the large Palladian house is composed of separate, symmetrical blocks. The main house (A) with a large portico in the middle and a tower at each end is similar to Wilton House, designed nearly one hundred years before by Inigo Jones. The wings (B) at each end are linked to the main house by, in this case, enclosed corridors (C). The second façade, based on the main part of Kedleston Hall, Derbyshire, shows a Palladian frontage in greater detail. The portico (D) has a plain triangular pediment supported on columns, themselves upon a base broken by arches, with the entrance up the stairs (E) on either side. The base (F) has rusticated masonry running the full width of the house, while the taller first floor (G) is the piano nobile and contains the state apartments. Further rooms are above distinguished by the row of square windows (H) while the top is finished off with a cornice (I) which was one of the few areas of decoration on these otherwise plain fronts.*

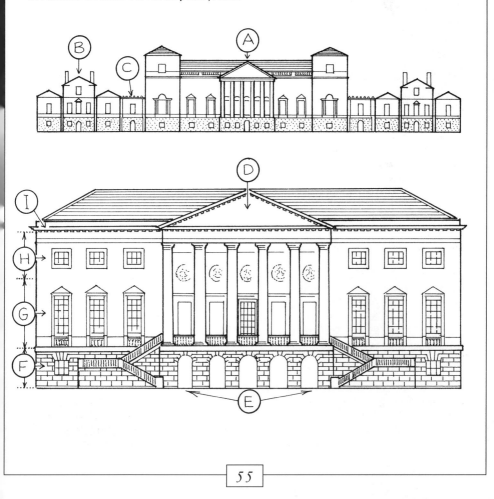

identified by a long line of tall rectangular windows, while if there were further rooms above, they would use smaller square windows. Most significant was the portico, a huge triangular pediment supported on columns, which acted as an enormous storm porch marking the main entrance to the house which was reached up a grand staircase below.

To the viewer Wanstead and its successors must have seemed dramatically different from existing houses. Gone were the flowing, undulating lines of the Baroque mansions and the stout, tall Dutch style houses; now plain, refined horizontal blocks with temple-like centrepieces were the order of the day for the gentleman of taste. Their beauty lay in the strict adherence to the rules of proportion, with decoration limited to carvings along the cornice and the top of the columns. The façade of these houses was also composed of individual blocks, so for instance the wing at one end of a mansion would make a perfectly proportioned house for a lesser gentleman or just a vertical section would make a refined Georgian town house!

FIG 4.5: KEDLESTON HALL, DERBYSHIRE: *Although the main body of the house was built in the Palladian style this south front and some of the principal rooms were completed by Robert Adam in a Neo Classic style. The typical arrangement of windows with a piano nobile above the rusticated base is still there, but the centre section with its projecting columns surmounted by statues, recessed niches, decorative medallions and garlands harks back to the Baroque influence. Crucially this centrepiece is based on an actual Roman triumphal arch rather than upon Palladio's designs.*

FIG 4.6: SHUGBOROUGH, STAFFORDSHIRE: *A Neo Classic façade but with evidence of two previous styles showing through. The three-storey main block is a Restoration house (similar to the elevation in fig 3.4) built in the 1690s, onto which wings were added either side in a Palladian style some fifty years later. With further alterations though the façade had become disjointed, so Samuel Wyatt redesigned it in the 1790s with a large, flat-topped portico and a balustrade running at the same level along the façade. This emphasised the horizontal lines which were a key component of a Classical house and held together the various elements from which the front was composed.*

Palladio also gave the architects of the day plans for other forms of houses, of which two proved particularly popular. A square plan with porticos on one or all four sides and a central dome above was the basis for Chiswick House, while a main rectangular block with individual wings linked by a colonnade or corridor inspired buildings like Kedleston Hall.

⌖ NEO CLASSICAL HOUSES

The new generation of architects who appeared in the mid 18th century found strict adherence to Palladio's pattern book too limiting. They wanted to be more imaginative and creative and it became acceptable to look to other periods in history for inspiration. This became easier thanks to archaeology.

Up to now houses were based on Renaissance interpretations or simply guesses at to what a Roman house would have looked like. For instance Palladio thought that each one had a portico on the front, so Campbell and his followers in their quest for historic accuracy stuck them on every building. It was only as the societies which these architects and their patrons helped to establish started to fund excavations in places like Pompeii that it became clear that Roman houses did not have porticos on the front. The new architects increasingly bypassed Palladio's works and went straight to these new archaeological sources for their inspiration.

At the same time Nicholas Revett and James Stuart produced the first accurate drawings of Ancient Greek buildings in Athens. Although the limited range of Greek forms did not immediately appeal to architects craving greater variety, as a replacement for Palladianism, they did add Greek Orders and detailing to their increasing architectural palette. The country houses which used these newly discovered Roman and Greek forms, from the 1760s onwards, are labelled Neo (New) Classical.

Another difference between Neo Classical houses and the previous Palladian buildings is a return to more playful use of Ancient architecture. Robert Adam, the most prolific country house architect of this period, believed that the Romans themselves had bent the rules, and he set about adding, as the Baroque architects had previously done, a sense of movement and space to his façades. Features to look out for are curved bay windows, flat domes, columns standing proud of the front and shallow arched recesses. However, Adam and other Neo Classical architects despised the Baroque use of flamboyant

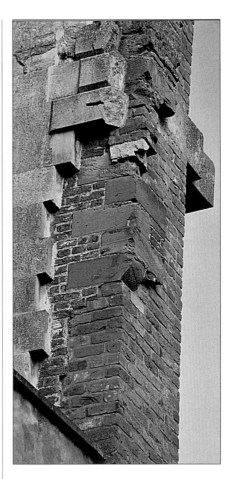

FIG 4.7: WITLEY COURT, WORCESTERSHIRE: *This now ruined country house was originally a brick Jacobean house which was later remodelled in a Classical style and clad in stone. Here where some of the stone cladding has fallen away you can see the earlier brick with its stone corner pieces (quoins). Note that the slightly larger bricks to the right side are later ones used to support the ruined wall (earlier bricks will tend to be thinner and more irregular in size).*

decoration to hide the function of the building beneath and houses in this period tend to be plain or even stark in appearance.

Most Palladian houses still used brick – although in a wider choice of colours and improved quality – or stone for the walls, with the shallow roof hidden behind a fairly plain parapet. Chimneys were no longer for showing off and were hidden or disguised to complement the design. After 1750 there was a move against leaving brick exposed and it tends to be covered in stucco (a plaster or cement coating) or clad in stone or even slate, as was the case at Shugborough where the earlier stucco would not adhere properly. For those who could not afford or did not wish to build a completely new house, it became common to have their brick façades reclad in these more fashionable materials and at the same time pop a few of the latest Classical details and perhaps an impressive portico upon the front. It is often only during building work or if they fall into a ruined state that you can see the original surface beneath.

Layout of the Houses

Throughout the 18th century there was an increased demand for space. The house would have to hold art works brought back from Continental travels, a library for a growing collection of books, a wider range of rooms for entertaining guests, and more specialist areas for the production and preparation of food. New houses were built, sometimes on new sites away from the original village, or in the same place but the owner would have the surrounding hovels removed to improve his view. Alternatively, older ones might be extended maybe more than once as the owner's wealth and status grew. Only the old Tory squires and repressed Catholic families, deprived of the incomes that came with holding office, had to make do with their old compact stone and brick piles, a situation that thankfully has saved many Tudor and Jacobean houses in their near original state for us to enjoy today.

One feature of the layout of Palladian and Neo Classical houses that was almost universal was to have the state apartments on a raised ground floor, the

FIG 4.8: *Four layouts of 18th century country houses with the shaded areas showing the possible position of the service rooms. (A) has two wings in line with the front of the house, while (B) has the popular plan for the larger house with four linked pavilions. (C) has the service rooms in a separate building which could be linked by a passage or even a tunnel, while in (D) a courtyard to the north of the house allows the sun to shine on the other three faces of the more compact country house.*

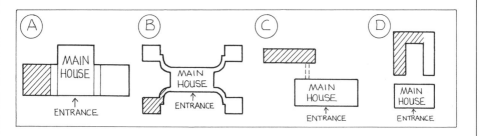

FIG 4.9: NOSTELL PRIORY, WEST YORKSHIRE: *The main house to the right is connected to the pavilion on the left by means of the single-storey corridor in the middle. Despite its attractive façade this pavilion housed the kitchen and service rooms (note the chimney at the top). The house was planned to look similar to fig 4.8 (B) – but, as you will find all over the country, such projects were frequently left incomplete, with just one or two wings rather than the intended four.*

piano nobile. Rather than being reserved for visiting dignitaries, they were now opened up at parties so that guests could parade through them admiring the art works and sculpture. They also provided more of a headache for the architects – who increasingly by the second half of the 18th century were professionals with their own practices. Not only did they have to include a wider range of rooms behind a façade that was limited by strict architectural rules laid down by Palladio and the Ancients, but also the size of the state apartments had to be in the correct

Classical proportions and the very plan of the house symmetrical! As a result a number of designs evolved, to get as near to fulfilling these requirements as possible for whatever the size of house.

For the larger house a main block with separate pavilions at each side connected by corridors or just an open colonnaded passage (a row of columns) proved ideal. The family and guests could be fed and entertained in the main house before retiring to the bedchambers on or above the piano nobile or in one of the pavilions. At the same time the odours and noises

FIG 4.10: *An imaginary plan of a compact country house with a separate courtyard containing the service rooms.*

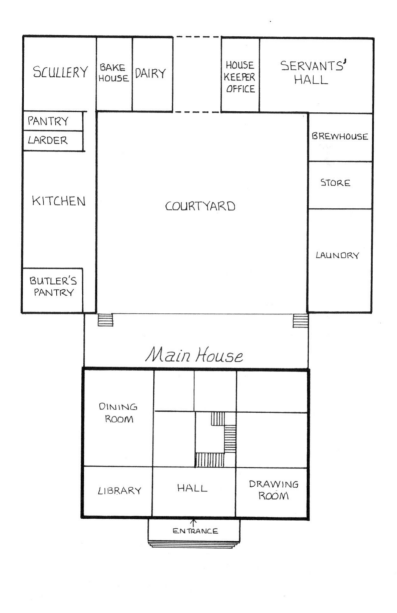

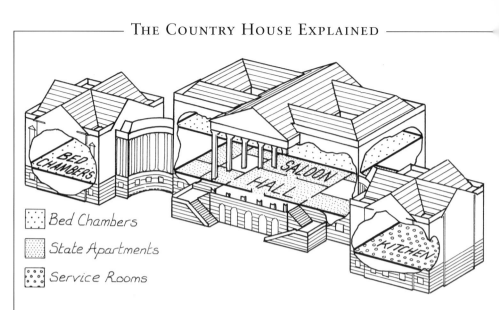

: Bed Chambers

State Apartments

Service Rooms

FIG 4.11: *A cut out view of a Palladian house. The hall and the saloon behind it form the axis of the house with as near as possible symmetrical arrangement of rooms off either side. Above these state apartments could be found bed chambers although some further family or guest rooms might be located in a wing. The kitchen is kept in a wing to reduce the fire and odour risk, although some store rooms like the cellar or butler's pantry would remain in the basement of the main house.*

FIG 4.12: **TATTON PARK, CHESHIRE:** *This mansion was rebuilt in stages by Samuel and Lewis Wyatt from 1780-1813 in the Neo Classic style. The recessed shallow arches above the outer windows, the swag motifs in the centre and the lack of decoration around the windows are typical features of houses from this period.*

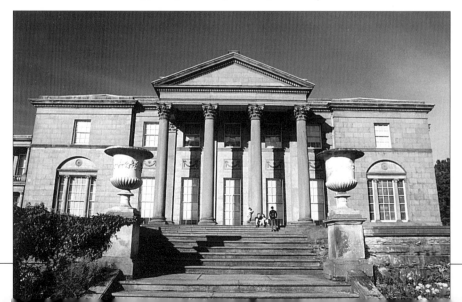

from the service rooms in another pavilion were kept at bay thanks to air passing across the corridor or passage which linked them, although the diners were increasingly likely to receive their food cold (see fig 4.8B and 4.11).

Most medium and smaller country houses were still built as a rectangular block. Some retained the 17th century habit of siting the service rooms in the basement, off a corridor running along the length of the house, with bedchambers on the first floor above the piano nobile. Increasingly, separate ranges of buildings for the service rooms were laid out, perhaps set back from the front, off to one side, or forming a courtyard at the rear of the house. These tended to be closer to the dining room so there may have been some heat in their meals but the owner's attempt to recreate a perfect scene from Ancient Rome or Greece could suddenly have an unwelcome carbuncle growing out of one side!

Another distinctive but limited plan type was a square layout with a central domed room. This perfect piece of symmetrical and proportional planning was used to great dramatic effect at Chiswick House (see fig 4.2) and Mereworth Castle, but its inflexibility in the size and layout of the rooms and the difficulty in accommodating service rooms, especially if the house was to be viewed on all four sides, limited its popularity.

Exterior Details

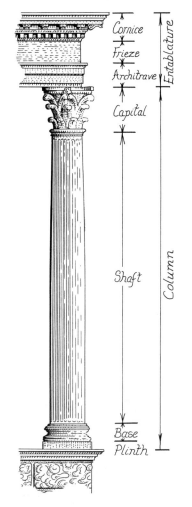

FIG 4.13: *A Classical column (in the Corinthian Order) listing the parts from which it is composed. Although the various Orders had differing proportions and detailing, it is the style of the capital that easily distinguishes one from another (see figs 4.14 to 4.17). The crude method I use to remember the principal Orders is: the DORIC looks Dull or bORIng; the Ionic looks like a capital 'I', and you go 'COR!' when you see the elaborate CORinthian! The shaft could be plain or fluted (vertical grooves are shown in this example) except for the Tuscan which was always plain.*

FIG 4.14: *Two columns in the Corinthian Order. Although first used by the Greeks, it was more popular with the Romans and hence it appears in England with the first Renaissance houses in the 16th century. These elaborate examples are from a gateway designed by Hawksmoor in 1723 for the entrance to Blenheim Palace from Woodstock.*

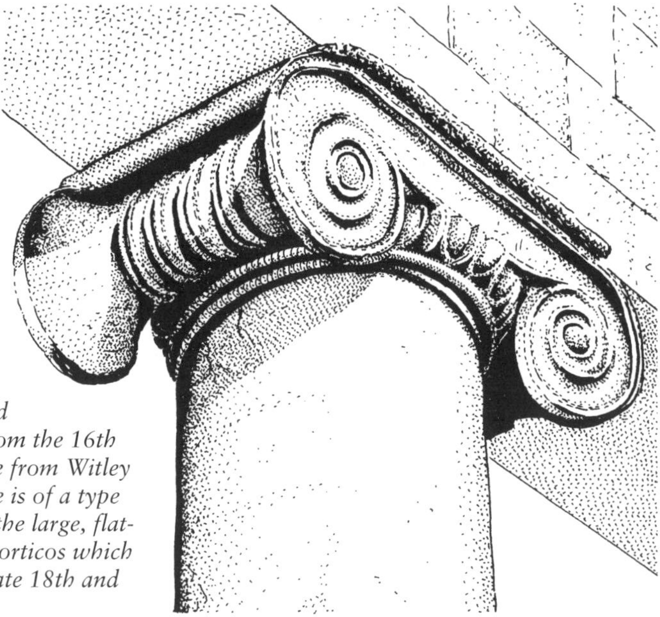

FIG 4.15: *The capital of a column in the Ionic Order. This distinctive design composed of two parallel scrolls was used by Greeks and Romans alike and again appears here from the 16th century. This example from Witley Court, Worcestershire is of a type commonly found on the large, flat-topped Neo Classic porticos which were popular in the late 18th and early 19th century.*

FIG 4.16: *The Composite Order, as the name suggests, is a mix of the Corinthian and its acanthus leaves with Ionic scrolls above. It can look very similar to the Corinthian but the scrolls should be larger on the Composite and there will be the band of egg-shaped details running between them. This order was a Roman creation and can be found on Tudor houses onwards.*

FIG 4.17 (A) and (B): *The Doric Order is divided into Greek and Roman styles. (A) was the first Order used by the Greeks and their version is easily recognisable as the shaft rests directly on the plinth as in this example from Shugborough, Staffordshire (see fig 10.18). The tiny dots on the underside of the cornice at the top are a common detail copied by architects from Ancient Greek examples. Rather than being meaningless decoration though, it is now believed that they were carved by Greek masons in imitation of the wooden pegs which held the earliest Greek temples together, when they were made of timber! The Roman Doric (B) has a ring below the capital and unlike the Greek version it rests upon a base. This example from Brodsworth Hall, South Yorkshire, with the plain entablature above and an unfluted column, is virtually identical to the Tuscan Order.*

FIG 4.18: CHISWICK HOUSE, LONDON: *A detail from the beautifully detailed cornice which runs around the top of the walls and portico.*

FIG 4.19: KEDLESTON HALL, DERBYSHIRE: *A detail from the south front designed by Robert Adam. He is notable as the first architect to really design a whole house from the exterior down to interior details and he formed a distinct style which still carries his name today. Here the projecting columns and recessed arch niches add movement to an otherwise flat frontage, while the medallions and a frieze of swags are popular Neo Classic decorations.*

FIG 4.20: *Sash windows were almost universally used in the 18th century. Their ability to be opened to any size at the top or bottom revolutionised the ventilation of rooms in the same way as air conditioning has in modern offices. Sash windows of this period have increasingly thinner glazing bars and have their outer frame recessed and often hidden behind the wall's outer surface. This was due to building regulations, which during the 18th century progressively recessed the wooden frames into the wall to reduce the chance of it catching fire if the neighbouring property went up in flames.*

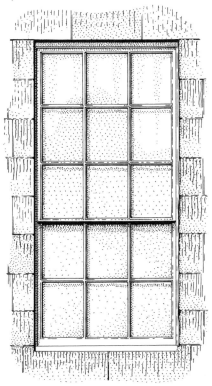

FIG 4.21: NOSTELL PRIORY, WEST YORKSHIRE: *A square sash window from within the rusticated base which ran along the lower part of the wall. Note the shutters which are closed inside. They were usually fitted in the sides but could pull up from a box in the window sill and were used for extra insulation, protection from sunlight falling on delicate fabrics and as a guard against intruders.*

FIG 4.22: CHISWICK HOUSE, LONDON: *A Venetian window with a tall arched centre panel flanked by lower rectangular ones was a very popular style on Palladian and Neo Classic houses.*

FIG 4.23: STOWE HOUSE, BUCKINGHAMSHIRE: *One of the pavilions at the end of the south front which were designed by Robert Adam in 1771. It features the shallow blank arches, decorative garlands and round medallions that were characteristic of this period.*

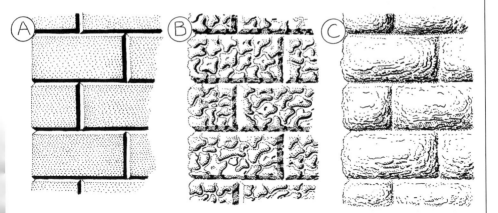

FIG 4.24: *Rusticated masonry could either be flat with channelled grooves (A) or left with a rough hewn finish (or simulated to give the appearance of this) as if it had been cut out of the very rock the house was built on (although it never actually was).*

FIG 4.25: **TATTON PARK, CHESHIRE:** *A panel with a garland, in this case of oak leaves, held by ribbons tied in a bow was a common Neo Classic motif.*

The owners of Exemplar Hall have during the 18th century made few changes to the main house, other than to give it a Classical makeover and stick a portico on the front. They have, however, dramatically changed its surroundings. A new wing with extra accommodation has been added on the foundations of the entrance to the stable block in the previous view. A courtyard in the foreground houses service rooms and stables while the emphasis of the house is now geared towards the garden at the rear.

The previous lord of the manor bought up the old village properties, cleared them out of the way and had a picturesque landscape garden laid out complete with temples and ruins. The old stream, which in the medieval and Tudor views fed the fishponds behind the house, has now been flooded to form a lake over which a Classical style bridge stands. The old medieval chapel which stood to the left of the house fell into disrepair and has been removed, with daily prayers now being taken in one of the state apartments. The owner of the house has renovated the parish church next door in a Classical style with private pews within for him and his family when they join the estate workers for Sunday service. Many of the villagers, though, who relocated to the small mill town which is developing beyond the top left of the picture, resented the long walk to service and now have their own chapel.

The period of intense building and gardening represented in this view of Exemplar Hall was to slow down in the last decades of the 18th century due to war with firstly America and then France. When stability returned there were new gentlemen, rich on commercial and industrial profit, entering the ranks of the aristocracy while the search for a suitable national style and influences from our increasing Empire combined to change the face of the country house in its last and most glorious period of development.

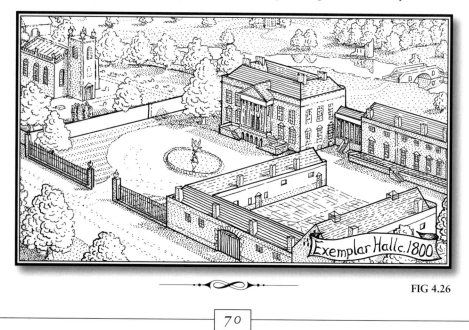

FIG 4.26

CHAPTER 5

Empire and Industry

—··◄∞►··—

REGENCY, VICTORIAN AND EDWARDIAN HOUSES

1800 - 1914

FIG 5.1: CAPESTHORNE HALL, CHESHIRE: *At first glance the brick exterior with ogee-shaped caps upon square towers, Dutch gables and mullioned windows looks like a Jacobean mansion. The arched veranda across the front and the lack of a central entrance porch is the only sign that it may not be all it seems. It is in fact a house of 1719 which was rebuilt in 1837 by Edward Blore in a pseudo Jacobean style. It is often only on a closer inspection of the details like brickwork and windows that a Victorian revival style house can be told apart from a genuine building of that period (see fig 5.17).*

The French Revolution and subsequent war with France heralded in a period of change, although it started as one of resistance to change on the part of the aristocracy. The threat of Napoleon saw the

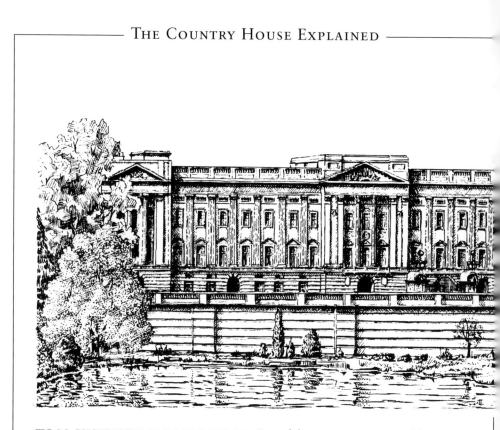

FIG 5.2: BUCKINGHAM PALACE, LONDON: *One of the great monuments of the patriotic Regency period dating from 1825-1830. It was in fact a rebuilding of the existing Buckingham House by John Nash for George IV, whose notoriety for extravagance was well founded. In 1913, the east frontage (shown above) was redesigned by Sir Aston Webb.*

country, severed from Europe, become fiercely patriotic, and a spate of national monuments, including Buckingham Palace, Trafalgar Square, the National Gallery and the British Museum, appeared in the capital. Enlightened thoughts and sensibility were quickly replaced by hard commercial facts and industrial ingenuity, to which even the old landed families had succumbed by the 1830s. In addition to their income from agricultural rents, which had supported the needs of their predecessors, there was now the profit from mines, mills and factories (often built on their country estates); from railways, canals, docks and shipping; or from investments in stocks and shares and rent from urban developments.

Despite the wealth the gentry amassed it became increasingly easy to lose it all. Huge sums were spent on a daughter's dowry, ever more grand houses, running election campaigns, maintaining a hunt (and receiving lower rents as compensation for damage done to fields and boundaries), gambling,

Revolution and revolt throughout the first half of the century had awoken them to the need to take more notice of the general populace in order to hang onto power and hence their fortunes. They were the cultural leaders of their day and passed their moral codes down to an aspiring middle class especially through public schools. The ideal gentleman would be a devout Christian and a good landlord, could be a supporter of the arts and improvements in health and education, but above all would be a faithful husband and family man.

On a realistic note many had lost interest in industry and commerce, with which their fathers had made their fortunes, so they entered political service but were more likely to be seen enjoying themselves hunting, shooting, smoking and playing billiards. Rather than collecting classical artefacts the 19th century gentleman would fill his rooms with antique furniture, family paintings, Persian rugs and houseplants while exotic trees from around the world adorned his garden. He could also succumb to the new national obsession with history. Less was being written about innovation and more about the past, especially the perceived highly religious and moral Middle Ages. The search for a national identity had focused on an isolationist mystical world of valiant knights and worthy craftsmen. It was probably as much a reaction against machines and a fear of the new than a quest for the origins of English democracy.

The Victorians had found Merry Old England on their doorstep and an Empire that was the envy of all other nations. Now at home they transferred the architecture from a favourite period or foreign country onto their houses.

especially horse racing, and entertaining shooting parties. Yet those from the lower ranks who had made a fortune still aspired to join the aristocracy and you could only begin to be recognised as such by the governing class if you had a country estate. Some married into old families, others bought names and titles or built their house in an antique style to imply a long lineage. The old landed gentry on the whole though protected their family inheritance, they avoided splitting their estates among siblings and were selective in who they married. The few properties that did become available to the up and coming gentleman were being sold off due to debts or when the family line expired.

By the middle of the 19th century the image of aristocrats was changing.

Style of the Houses

Up to this point country houses have fitted into fairly neat periodic groupings, but from the late 18th century all hell breaks loose and a medley of styles appear to burst onto the scene. As previously mentioned, designers of Neo Classical houses found their inspiration direct from archaeology and did not restrict themselves to one particular source, thus it became acceptable for architects to use styles other than those from Ancient Greece and Rome. At first this appeared as decoration adorning existing building types, but it developed to affect the very structure of the country house.

At the same time there had been a growing appreciation of the picturesque. This had started with the classical scenes painted by artists like Claude and Poussin, which featured grassy meadows rolling down to lakes bordered by rugged mountains and waterfalls, with ruined castles, temples and towers as the focal point or in the background. These inspired the landscape gardens of the 18th century and the follies and garden buildings that acted as eye catchers within these schemes. By the close of the century some of the country houses that they surrounded were being designed as if they had been plucked from one of these pictures. This freed architects from the strict rules of symmetry and proportion, so that picturesque houses could use a variety of textures and shapes and most notably could be asymmetric. There were also important associations to be made with the choice of style and site, for instance a castle built on top of a rocky outcrop implied power, strength and solidity, and inspired awe, which was more important than the architectural detail when viewed closer at hand.

Another factor which affected houses was improved construction materials and methods associated with the Industrial Revolution. Architecture starts to blend with engineering in this period. For instance, behind the stone or brick façade of Victorian country houses, a frame of iron posts and girders may be hiding! New products like large panes of glass for windows appeared, oil and then gas replaced candles, while running

FIG 5.3: *A symmetrical façade to the left and an asymmetrical one to the right.*

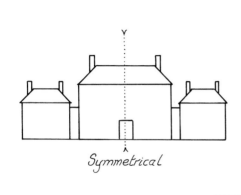

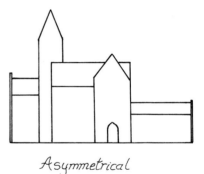

FIG 5.4: NETHER WINCHENDON HOUSE, BUCKINGHAMSHIRE: *There are medieval and Tudor parts, including some of the chimneys, but this house received a Regency makeover in the latest Gothick fashion, which included facing much of the timber framed parts in stone. Note the period features like the stout little pointed windows with Y-shaped glazing bars, battlements and a balcony between the two nearest towers.*

water, bathrooms and flushing toilets became commonplace in the 19th century. Even electricity was supplied to a few forward-thinking individuals' houses.

In this section I have grouped these various styles together in date order along with illustrations of their details. This will hopefully facilitate identification, so that a 19th century imitation may be more easily distinguished from the earlier style on which it is based, and add some logic to this bewildering yet glorious range of Regency and Victorian houses.

▓ REGENCY STYLES

The period from 1790-1837, which is loosely termed Regency (although the Prince Regent only ruled as such during his father's illness between 1811 and 1820), is notable for a wide selection of styles, but these were mostly applied decoration onto existing house types rather than radically new structures. From now on it was even acceptable to mix a number of the different styles up in one house. Distinguishing features of the period include the use of stucco, usually painted white or cream, ironwork for decorative details, especially balconies, and flat pitched roofs made possible due to the wider availability of slate (the lightness of which allowed the angle of the roof to be lowered). Sash windows now appeared more graceful as inserting metal into the wooden glazing bars helped make them thinner.

look for are steeply pitched roofs with end gables, battlements along the top of these and parapets, pointed-arch windows with leaded lights and drip mouldings above, tall Tudor style chimneys and, if it has not been stripped off, a painted stucco finish.

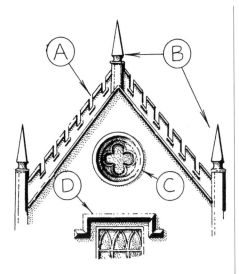

FIG 5.5: *A Regency Gothick gable in a stucco finish. The (A) raked battlements, (B) pinnacles, (C) quatrefoil (four circles interlocked) and (D) hood moulding above the window are typical features of this style.*

GOTHICK STYLE HOUSES: Gothick (the k at the end differentiating it from the later Victorian Gothic) made its first notable reappearance in house design at Strawberry Hill in Twickenham, the home of Horace Walpole (youngest son of the first Prime Minister, Robert Walpole). His restyling of this house from 1750 was a breakthrough in its asymmetrical design and use of fairly accurate Gothic details, which reflected the growing interest in romantic ruins of abbeys and castles. From 1790 a number of architects produced new Gothick country houses with this more irregular layout, though for many this developing national style was applied just to existing properties or new extensions. Details to

FIG 5.6: *A small, stout Gothick window with Y-shaped tracery. Later Gothic windows tend to have slender proportions or are rectangular with a pointed decoration above them.*

FIG 5.7: LOWTHER CASTLE, CUMBRIA: *At first glance this appears to be a very convincing castle, but look again and a house emerges. Note that the central block has tall windows with smaller square ones above, and that there are pavilions at each end of the building, just like a Palladian mansion, while the main body is reminiscent of Wollaton Hall (fig 2.8), which itself was inspired by castle architecture. The theatrical arrangement of four sets of receding twin tower features in the middle, the perfect symmetry and the regularly positioned windows confirm that it is a 19th century creation. It was built by Robert Smirke from 1806-11, but the Lowther family moved out in the 1930s and it was partly demolished in 1957 leaving just the shell.*

CASTLE STYLE HOUSES: Another popular nationalistic style of the Regency and Victorian period, which peaked during the first half of the 19th century, was the castle. Robert Adam gave castle-like designs acceptability in his belief that they were direct descendants of the architecture the Romans had brought with them to these shores and hence linked the Ancient World and Britain together in one. It is also true that castles had never gone away, as many genuine ones after the turbulent times of the 15th century and the later Civil War had been converted into residences. Now, though, completely new houses in the style of castles were rising all over the country, partly inspired by the ruins which featured in the gentry's travels or books and by romantic tales from the likes of Walter Scott. The owners may also have wanted to reassert their social status in this period of workers' discontent and at the same time give the impression that their family had ancient roots.

Distinguishing a genuine castle from these new ones can be tricky at a glance. The things to look at are, firstly, the general composition of the building – is it all of the same, well-finished stone as in the case of a new one, or is it made up of different ages of material? Is it militarily correct with curtain walls and earthworks surrounding a courtyard or keep as you would expect in a genuine castle, or does it look as if it has been designed by an architect, with towers sprinkled for aesthetic value or an impressive symmetrical front? Lots of large windows which would be a military disaster in battle can be a give away, although these can be seen – knocked through – in genuine castles, though rarely with the regularity of a mock one. A variation of this style is SCOTTISH BARONIAL which was popular North of the Border. Its distinguishing features include tall outside walls surmounted by small corner turrets and towers with pointed caps.

FIG 5.8: CRONKHILL, SHROPSHIRE: *Its stark geometric shapes almost give it a 20th century feel, but it was the creation of John Nash in 1802 and was inspired by the Italianate buildings in the pictures of Claude.*

EXOTIC STYLES: Increased travel and trade, with a wider range of ever distant countries and new colour illustrations of their architecture, inspired some of the upper classes to remodel their homes in exotic styles. As was typical of this period they tend to manifest themselves in details added on to an English styled house and the only time you are likely to find these fashions accurately represented is on the smaller garden buildings and follies around the main house.

Italianate villa style houses featured in the paintings which inspired the Picturesque movement. Towers offset to one end, low-pitched roofs with deep overhanging eaves, and arcades of arched openings are identifying details.

Napoleon's presence in Egypt had led to French archaeologists uncovering and drawing the great monuments they found. The Egyptian style which was inspired by these discoveries is characterised by thick round columns with lotus leaf capitals, walls which lean in at the top, and large concave eaves.

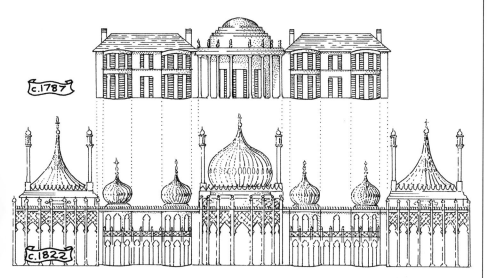

FIG 5.9: THE ROYAL PAVILION, SUSSEX: *This outrageous blend of Indian styled elements was designed by John Nash for the Prince Regent from 1815-22. At its heart though is a far more conventional Neo Classic villa which was expanded for the supposedly bankrupt Prince and his lover Mrs Fitzherbert. The left-hand part of the top view was the original house onto which was built the central dome and duplicate wing to the right in 1787. The dotted lines show its position within the Royal Pavilion's later incarnation.*

East European and Asian architectural styles, especially from India and China, inspired a number of houses, most notably the Prince Regent's Royal Pavilion at Brighton. Onion-shaped domes, exotic window and door styles, and chimneys disguised as minarets cover what was until 1815 a modest Neo Classic house. However, Oriental taste had more influence on the interiors of country houses.

NEO CLASSIC AND GREEK REVIVAL STYLES: Despite becoming the chosen taste of our arch enemy Napoleon, Classical architecture was still prominent in large country house design during this Regency period. The latest Classical designs were influenced more and more by the discoveries from Greece, and the temple – which was seen as Ancient Greek architecture in its purest form – features in part on many houses from this date. The exteriors were also devoid of decoration, and thus appear as plain, rectangular blocks, often with a flat or triangular roofed portico or colonnade projecting from the façade. The freestanding columns which supported them are structural rather than ornamental, and in keeping with the rest of the house tend to be in the simple Greek Orders of Doric and Ionic (see figs 4.15 and 4.17A).

FIG 5.10: WITLEY COURT, WORCESTERSHIRE: *The immense portico with a flat top and Greek Ionic columns is a Neo Classic feature often added to houses in this period. In its now ruined state you can see the earlier 18th century bow front behind it while to the side are Italianate arched windows from a later Victorian restyling.*

FIG 5.11: SHUGBOROUGH, STAFFORDSHIRE: *The garden front of this late 17th and 18th century house (see fig 4.6) had the central bow extension added from 1803-6 in a Neo Classic style. Period details include the swags and tails around the oval window at the top, the plain pilasters (flat, rectangular columns slightly raised from the wall) and the trellised verandas either side. The French doors opening directly onto the garden were also a new development, although the glass and frame of these examples looks later.*

When Queen Victoria came to the throne in 1837 Neo Classical architecture was falling from favour in country house design, despite its popularity for public buildings especially in the north.

▦ VICTORIAN AND EDWARDIAN STYLES

The inspiration for Victorian and Edwardian country house design came from many historic and geographic sources, of which the most notable ones are listed below. In general brick comes back into fashion, a wider range of materials allows the pitch and covering of roofs to vary according to style, and asymmetrically placed towers appear, often used to house tanks which provided running water for all those new closets and bathrooms. Now with larger panes of glass available the sash

FIG 5.12: *A Victorian sash window with no glazing bars to obstruct the view!*

window could virtually dispense with glazing bars and give uninterrupted views across the property. These clear windows are one of the few ways to tell a Victorian French chateau, mock Tudor or Elizabethan styled building from a genuine one, although caution has to be taken as these later windows could always be inserted into an older house.

GOTHIC REVIVAL: The 1830s were a time of intense religious debate centred on groups at Oxford, Cambridge and London as the Church of England faced up to an identity crisis. This in part had been caused by the Catholic Emancipation Act of 1829 which had removed most of the restrictions dating back to the fanatical anti-papal years of the 16th and 17th centuries. One Catholic convert who rose to prominence in this period was Augustus Welby Northmore Pugin, who in a series of books enthusiastically promoted Gothic architecture. He argued that in order for buildings to have moral value they should not hide their function and structure and that they should use natural materials – points of view which had a dramatic influence upon Victorian architects.

Pugin and others saw the Middle Ages, in particular the 14th century, as a time of high religious morality and the early buildings in this new Gothic Revival style use forms from this period for inspiration. There was no stucco hiding the basic materials, brick could once again be on show. Medieval traceried windows, tall, rather slender towers and an asymmetrical layout are distinguishing features of early Gothic Revival houses.

From the 1850s to 70s there was a move to a more muscular form of

FIG 5.13: *A Gothic style gable above a window with polychromatic (many colours) brickwork and decorative roof tiles with a patterned ridge, typical of the mid to late Victorian period.*

FIG 5.14: ABBERLEY, WORCESTERSHIRE: *A Gothic style clock tower built in 1883 – said locally to have been erected so that the owner from a new aristocratic family could look down upon the land belonging to his neighbour, the Earl of Dudley.*

Gothic with dramatic decoration and stout towers, less influenced by the English Middle Ages and more by Continental sources. However, the most distinguishing feature of houses of this date is the use of polychromatic brickwork where most commonly red brick walls were broken by bands and patterns in lighter or darker colours.

FIG 5.15: BULSTRODE PARK, BUCKINGHAMSHIRE: *The stocky Gothic tower in red brick with diagonal patterns is typically mid Victorian. This muscular looking building with spires, gables and battlements was built from 1861-70.*

TUDOR, ELIZABETHAN AND JACOBEAN STYLES: Another popular inspirational source for country house building was the 16th century and early 17th century. Tudor red brick houses and the imposing Elizabethan and Jacobean prodigy houses found fervent ground in

FIG 5.16: *A Dutch style gable with diaper patterns in the brickwork, typical of a mock Jacobean house dating from the mid Victorian period.*

FIG 5.17: *Sometimes it is only the detail that enables you to distinguish between a mock period house and the genuine article. The photograph on the left shows Victorian brickwork which is of a regular size and is in good condition with fine mortar joints. The right-hand photograph shows irregular, hand made bricks from a 16th century building which are badly worn and have wider joints.*

this patriotic period (see fig 5.1). Even detail down to the strapwork decoration the Elizabethans so loved was copied, although the varying height of windows depending on which floor the state rooms were in the original houses was not usually replicated. Sometimes it is only in the regular size and equality of finish of Victorian bricks over hand made Tudor ones that you can tell these houses apart from the originals.

ITALIANATE STYLES: If you were not enticed to build your new house in one of these traditional fashions then the style of the Italian Renaissance may have done the trick. It allowed the owner plenty of the rich decoration which the Victorian so loved, and windows in which to show off the latest large panes of glass. Some Italianate houses were villa-like, having offset square towers with a low pyramid-shaped roof and a group of three

FIG 5.18 BRODSWORTH HALL, SOUTH YORKSHIRE: *This immaculate mid Victorian Italianate house features vases and a balustrade along the top, cornice and mouldings over the windows, French doors along the base but notably no Classical columns on this façade (freestanding columns were not favoured by Victorians). It also differs from most 17th and 18th century country houses in that we now have two roughly equal height floors with no visible basement or attic.*

FIG 5.19: *Two Italianate windows from Witley Court, Worcestershire, with their distinctive Romanesque (semi circular) arches.*

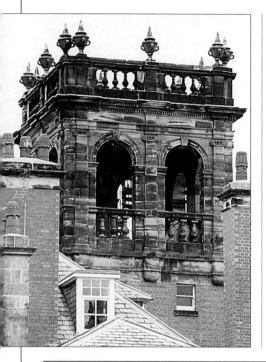

FIG 5.20: BIDDULPH GRANGE, STAFFORDSHIRE: *An Italianate styled tower.*

FIG 5.21: WADDESDON MANOR, BUCKINGHAMSHIRE: *Locals must have looked on amazed as this French chateau complete with a surrounding cloak of mature trees appeared on top of a once barren hill in rural Buckinghamshire during the 1880s. It was built for Baron Ferdinand de Rothschild, one member of the large Austrian banking family whose various relations purchased five other properties within the county, due to its close proximity to London and excellent hunting. The Baron used various 17th century sources for inspiration although it was the architect Destailleur, who had himself restored numerous chateaux, who put the mix together in what appears to English eyes a very authentic composition.*

FIG 5.22: *This detail from an Edwardian building shows how the Queen Anne style houses with their bright white paintwork and carved brickwork made a pleasant change from the rather grim Gothic.*

windows below, and a low pitched roof with a large overhanging cornice projecting over the walls. Others could take the form of a large Classical house, with generally symmetrical façades, few if any columns, decorative parapets with vases and equal rows of windows.

FRENCH STYLE architecture became popular during the second half of the 19th century, inspired by the fashionable changes that were taking place in Paris under the reign of Napoleon III. This so called Second Empire style is usually recognisable by the use of mansard roofs which have a shallow top slope followed by a steep lower one (which could be concave or convex), and lines of dormer

windows. This allowed rooms to be put into the usually limited roof void and made them popular in urban buildings where space was at a premium. Out in the country the chateau with steeply angled roofed towers and Baroque type decoration also inspired a number of projects.

QUEEN ANNE STYLE can also be found towards the end of the century although it was predominantly an urban fashion. Despite its name it is based on 17th century houses with Dutch gables, dormer windows, carved brickwork and walls edged with stone quoins which were popular in the reign of Charles II and William and Mary. The white-painted balconies and window frames have a look that is very different from the pointed red brick Gothic mansions of the day.

OLD ENGLISH AND ARTS AND CRAFTS HOUSES: This final, very distinctive style of country house architecture found favour in the late Victorian and Edwardian period, especially in the hands of two great architects Richard Norman Shaw and Edwin Lutyens. Shaw designed a number of country houses in what was labelled Old English style, which were characterised by exaggerated tall brick chimneys and long sloping tiled roofs overhanging low walls. Mullioned windows filled with leaded glass were used, often making up long rows tucked right up under the eaves. The layout was asymmetrical but very cleverly controlled and further variety and authenticity came in the use of a variety of materials all in the same house. These more modest looking houses were a reaction against the huge Gothic and Italianate piles of previous decades and well suited the new gentlemen of the period.

FIG 5.23: WIGHTWICK MANOR, WEST MIDLANDS: *An Old English styled house, asymmetrical, with a timber frame exterior standing above a brick base.*

They obviously take inspiration from vernacular architecture, which was being championed during this period by the Arts and Crafts movement, in particular by William Morris. It was a time of great nostalgia, traditional pastimes were revived, the National Trust was formed

FIG 5.24: *Sets of incredibly tall chimneys joined together up their full height mark this out as a late Victorian or Edwardian house in the Old English or Traditional style.*

and *Country Life* was first published. This magazine played a large part in promoting the designs of a young Edwin Lutyens who continued this Traditional house style into the 20th century.

Although Lutyens soon turned to Classical architecture which had revived, at least in public buildings, during the short reign of Edward VII, the days of the country house were coming to a close.

FIG 5.25: WIGHTWICK MANOR:
Intricate carved timber demonstrates the high level of Victorian workmanship. Styles of text on a building can also help to date it.

Layout of the Houses

Although the exteriors may have seemed cluttered up with the past, the layout of the houses was new and reflected the changing social climate.

The piano nobile which dominated in the previous century is gone, and the main rooms are on the ground floor. The procession of state apartments is also a thing of the past with more informal rooms arranged in a less strictly symmetrical manner. Rooms were increasingly dedicated to a precise purpose in the 19th century, with breakfast, smoking, music and billiards rooms frequently appearing in the plan.

Freed from the restraints of symmetry

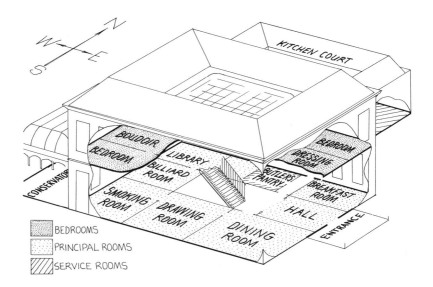

N
W E
S

KITCHEN COURT

BOUDOIR

BEDROOM

LIBRARY

BILLIARD ROOM

BEDROOM

DRESSING ROOM

CONSERVATORY

BUTLERS PANTRY

BREAKFAST ROOM

SMOKING ROOM

DRAWING ROOM

DINING ROOM

HALL

ENTRANCE

▨ BEDROOMS
░ PRINCIPAL ROOMS
▨ SERVICE ROOMS

FIG 5.26: *A cut out view of a Victorian country house with the principal rooms, now on the ground floor, dedicated to a more precise use. Upstairs are the bedrooms and dressing rooms, while the service rooms are in the separate kitchen court at the rear. Note that the central stairwell is top lit by a glass ceiling light. These more imaginative illuminating effects are a feature of 19th century houses.*

the layout could be more flexible depending on the style of house. Gothic buildings could sprawl out with no regular plan, Tudor and Elizabethan mansions might be set around a courtyard, while Italianate palaces were usually presented as a rectangular block. The awkward problem of where to site the service rooms was generally solved by building a courtyard or rear wing often to the north of the house (see fig 4.10). This meant that the food was nearer to the dining room than it had been when sited in the 18th century pavilions. As the courtyard or wing were not underneath the main house, as they had been in the basement service rooms which were still occasionally used, there was no restriction upon their size and arrangement of rooms. This was ideal bearing in mind the still numerous room types that the architect had to accommodate.

The picturesque landscape gardens which appeared to come right up to the house were by the Victorian period outdated and there was a return to terraces and flowerbeds which could now be viewed from fashionable French doors and verandas. Interest in nature and the foreign parts of our Empire fuelled a fashion for exotic plants and trees. The conservatories and greenhouses which were built to house them, often as a wing or even part of the structure of the house, are a distinctive feature of 19th century country houses.

Some forty years before this view is dated, the owner embarked on another face-lift and expansion of the property. The wing to the right of the picture was extended to create additional rooms for leisure and guest accommodation, a tower was constructed to hold the water tank and the service courtyard in the foreground was enlarged, with a walled kitchen garden just in the bottom right corner of the picture.

This was a time of great prosperity on the estate due to high agricultural returns, but by 1900 a sharp downturn in fortunes has resulted in the sale of much of the farm and parkland. At the same time the small mill town where the evicted villagers had resettled in our previous visit has expanded rapidly and new villas for the successful businessmen have encroached in the top and bottom left of the picture.

These are not promising times for Exemplar Hall, and the owner has to hope that things improve by the time his sole heir inherits the estate from him. Unfortunately the growing tide of social and political change and the repercussions of events in far off lands were to overtake this and many other country houses and bring the curtain down on the age of aristocratic rule.

FIG 5.27

CHAPTER 6

The Changing Fortunes of the Country House

On a sunny day in May 1869, upon a barren plain some 56 miles west of Ogden, Utah, USA, the final spike where two railroad tracks met was about to be driven home by Leland Stanford of the Central Pacific. His stroke with the hammer missed, but the eager telegrapher was already sending the message that the first transcontinental railway across America was complete. Now huge quantities of grain and livestock from the American West could be moved east by train and then, aided by breakthroughs in refrigeration, shipped abroad.

Back in England the landowners sitting in their country houses were basking in the warm glow of a Golden Age in farming, yet by the mid 1870s American imports, filling shortfalls in our production, were keeping the price of corn steady and then by the 1880s lowering it. The Agricultural Depression triggered by this and the effects of a general economic downturn meant reduced rents and income for the aristocracy. The last decades of the 19th century were also a period of change in matters of government with most males receiving the vote and county councils being formed, which had the effect of depriving the landed gentry of political power and the revenue it could guarantee. It is notable that Asquith, who became Prime Minister in 1908, was the first without a country seat!

The legislation passed in this period by Parliament had further crippling effects on country estates with the introduction of Death Duties in 1894, and higher rates of income and super tax in 1909.

Tragedy struck at Exemplar Hall one winter's day in 1917 when news reached the family that the young lord had been killed in action in a Flanders field. Here as with many country estates the loss of young men in World War I would have devastating effects. Exemplar's owner died shortly after the end of the conflict and as he left no heir and mounting debts it was sold off and became a private school. This was poorly run and by the time of the Second World War the property was in the hands of the armed forces as a training centre. After these hostilities the local town council purchased the site but the lack of maintenance had left the old hall unsafe and the majority of the building was demolished. Only the old kitchen courtyard was retained and has become offices while the remainder of the estate is now a public park. After all these years only the church and its surrounding boundary have survived from the original scene in 1400.

Although an imaginary tale, similar stories can be found all over the country of lost grand houses. Where I currently live three former stately homes have, in the last century, become a school, a council housing estate and a leisure centre. Virtually nothing remains of the buildings in these situations, although at other more rural sites the house may still stand if only as a brick or masonry shell. Ironically they have themselves become romantic ruins like the ones in Rome which may have inspired their original owners to build them in the first place! Despite the melancholy of their fallen glory, those disused houses that are open to the public are fascinating, as stripped of internal decoration their sometimes surprising construction methods and piecemeal development can be seen behind the apparently grand façade.

Thankfully many country houses have survived although often only through diversification into other fields like theme and wildlife parks, museums, and as locations for special or corporate events. Some still remain in the same family, while others are maintained by bodies like the National Trust and English Heritage. If you take the six Rothschild houses around Aylesbury in Buckinghamshire (see fig 5.21) as an example, one is now an RAF camp, one a hotel, one is owned by a religious group and another is a school, while the two remaining ones are open to the public through the National Trust.

Hopefully, after you have read the first part of this book, the outside of the country house will not appear quite as bewildering, and the explanation of the reasons behind the styles and structure, together with the listing of details from which a house may be dated, will enhance your visit. But now it is time to step through that grand portico or carved oak doorway and explore the interior …

FIG 6.1

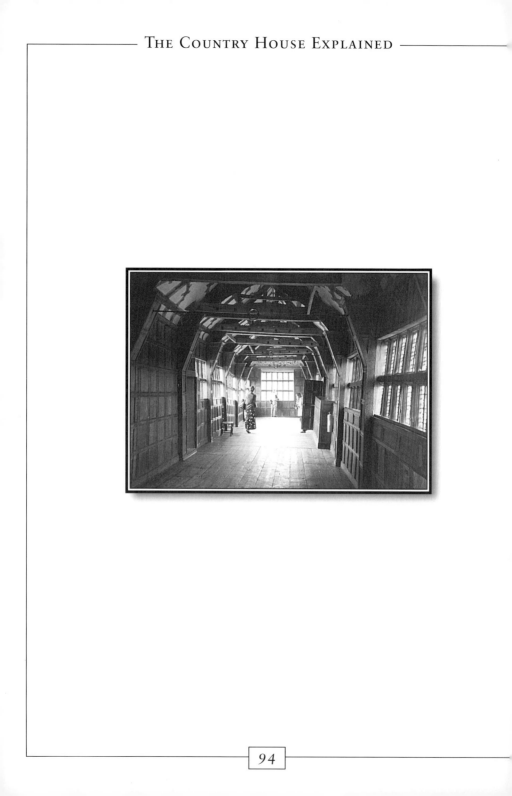

SECTION II

LOOKING INSIDE THE COUNTRY HOUSE

CHAPTER 7

Interior Structures

If the exterior of a country house was prone to fashionable tinkering by succeeding generations, then the interior was even more susceptible, to what could be regular and complete makeovers. For instance you may find a Tudor brick mansion still retaining its original façade despite some new trimmings and the odd extension, while inside the rooms could be a medley of later Baroque, Rococo, Neo Classical or Victorian Gothic styles. The interiors were personal and, reflecting the personality and lifestyle of each new owner, could be more opulent, exotic and outrageous than the public exterior of the house.

This greater individuality of interiors and the bewildering array of fittings and

FIG 7.1: One of the most popular designs with which to decorate wood panelling in the 16th century was 'linenfold', a rippling effect representing folded cloth.

furnishings that embellish them have led me to concentrate here on the main structures and uses of the rooms rather than on their contents, which are usually well covered in a house's own guidebook.

Before looking at the various rooms and their changing roles in a country house, this chapter explains how the main elements of a room were decorated and describes some of the period details from which they can be dated.

⌗ WALLS

Today most of our remaining houses from the Middle Ages are displayed showing the bare face of the materials from which they are constructed. This gives the false impression that the medieval world was a cold, colourless place, as in most cases the opposite is true.

Walls inside and out were at least whitewashed and often coloured, including timber frames, which only donned their familiar black coating thanks to zealous Victorians. The interior surfaces could be further decorated with ochre or red lines simulating masonry patterns, while wall hangings, usually of cloth painted in strong colours, were used to reduce draughts especially at the lord's end of the hall. Tapestries were a luxury of the very rich and only appear in country houses at the earliest in the 14th century. These wall coverings had the advantage that they could be packed up and taken with the owner's entourage when moving from house to house.

By the 16th century the owner was more likely to stay put in one splendid house and wood panelling covering the lower part or even the complete height of the wall became common. This was composed of frames with usually square

FIG 7.2: *Part of an early 17th century long gallery showing how the Renaissance had influenced the design of wood panelling. The traditional square panels are replaced by walls divided up into different sized sections with classical pilasters, arches and decorative strapwork (the pilasters characteristically angle inwards at the base). Jacobean houses are notable for their beautiful carving.*

FIG 7.3: WITLEY COURT, WORCESTERSHIRE: *A section of wall showing how the plaster was applied to the laths, projecting out of the left-hand side, and was then built up in layers before the moulding was applied.*

panels which could be decorated with carved scenes, figures or patterns. It acted not only as a decoration that could display great wealth, but also as an insulation barrier and one which, unlike cloth hangings, would not absorb food smells. By the 17th century classical designs in wood influenced by the Renaissance decorate many Jacobean houses while in later Restoration houses carving reached breathtaking delicacy in the hands of craftsmen like Grinling Gibbons, with intricate patterns of naturalistic themes framing or decorating panels.

By this time though, plastering the wall, which helped reduce the fire risk, was becoming fashionable. The plaster, which was made from lime or gypsum often with hair, straw or reed within to give it strength, was applied over wooden laths (thin strips of wood) which had been pinned to the wall. The surface was punctuated by mouldings made from plaster, stucco or even papier maché, which could form classically proportioned panels, cornices and decorative pieces. To protect these the lower section of the wall, known as the dado, might still be panelled or at least have a rail (dado rail) fitted along its upper edge where the rear of chairs (which were positioned around the edge of the room at this date) might rub.

The style of decorative mouldings changed over time from flamboyant Baroque shapes, which were still acceptable even in the strict Palladian houses, to, in the mid 18th century, Rococo. This was named after the French word *rocaille* which described the rocky encrustations which featured on the fashionable grottos of the time, and was distinguished by curves, shells and naturalistic features forming

FIG 7.4: *The left-hand interior view shows typical 16th century square panels (A). The panelling may sometimes reach the ceiling, or only run a third or halfway up, or as in this case just leave a short gap (B) at the top. The right-hand views shows an 18th century room in which its height matches its width, so a coffered ceiling (C) is inserted to lower the apparent height of the wall below. This is topped by a cornice (D) and decorated with rectangular moulded plaster panels (E), while the dado section (F) below is finished off with a dado rail (G) to protect the wall from the backs of chairs which typically lined the edge of the room at this time.*

asymmetrical patterns, usually in white and gold.

In the Neo Classic period of the late 18th and early 19th century, architects like Robert Adam, who created his own interior design style, were influenced by new Greek, Roman and Etruscan discoveries. Flatter and more delicate mouldings, with swags, vases, griffins and gold beads, decorated panels which were painted in more subdued pastel colours.

Wallpaper first became a popular covering in stately homes in the late 17th century. Increased trading with the Far East led to the importing of luxury hand-painted papers from China which featured scenes from nature, in particular bird and flower designs. Flock wallpaper,

made from leftover wool sprinkled on glued pattern areas of the paper, featured in some 18th century houses, while French papers with exotic scenes or simulated fabric patterns were still popular into the Victorian period. Fabrics were used as wall coverings, especially silk damasks, though even materials as diverse as leather still survive in some houses. As the plaster surface may not have been good enough, early coverings were glued onto canvas which was pinned to wall battens, until in the 19th century a smoother plaster surface could be achieved and wallpapers attached to it directly.

Curved walls are an interesting 18th century feature, either making an alcove or apse for a statue or forming a

FIG 7.5: *Three examples of plasterwork ceilings, typical of Elizabethan and Jacobean houses, in which the design was very prominent above the surface of the plaster.*

completely round room with a dome above, based on examples from the Ancient world. Columns were introduced for added grandeur, to control the apparent size of a room or to add movement. Robert Adam used these forms at Syon House, London, to form a double cube out of an originally longer room (see fig 8.7).

By the Victorian period it had become fashionable for furniture to be scattered around the room with tables and chairs arranged in intimate circles rather than up against the sides. As a result, walls with a full height hanging of paper or fabric and without the protective dado rail appear, although the rail and panels still remained fashionable.

The obsession with history in this period meant that rooms were often decorated in simulated Gothic, Classical, Italianate, French or Castle styles. The plain stone walls and black and white timbers the Victorian designers used in their fake Gothic halls may reinforce that rather misguided impression we tend to have of a colourless medieval world.

▨ CEILINGS

Ceilings did not exist in early medieval halls as the central hearth necessitated the roof being opened to the rafters although the trusses which supported it could be lavishly carved and decorated. The subsequent positioning of the chimney on a side wall permitted the

FIG 7.6: WOLLATON HALL, NOTTINGHAMSHIRE: *This Elizabethan prodigy house was inspired by medieval castles so an immense hall was built with decorated timber trusses above. Although similar to those used in later medieval halls, this features a flat wooden panelled ceiling inserted above the trusses, as by this time the hearth had been replaced by fireplaces.*

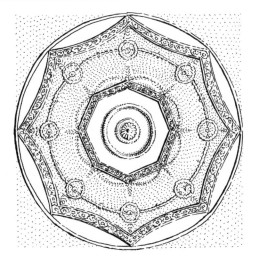

FIG 7.7: *The left-hand ceiling design is typical of that found in late 17th and early 18th century houses with a painting framed by oval, round or square mouldings which are still deep and decorated with Baroque motifs. The right-hand example is a late 18th century Robert Adams design which uses more delicate Neo Classic features and has a notably shallower relief.*

owner to insert a room above and therefore a ceiling, which to compensate for the loss of his elaborately carved timber roof could be decorated with raised plaster geometric patterns (see fig 7.5). Wooden laths were pinned to the underside of the floor joists and plaster applied over these. By the late 17th century skilled plasterers were creating Classical style ceilings with large oval or rectangular centrepieces featuring paintings surrounded by delicate flowers and swags (see fig 7.6).

Most of these ceilings were one colour with gilding as the paintings and elaborate plasterwork added enough interest. In Neo Classical and Adam interiors, though, the flatter mouldings they used needed more colour to lift them, and combinations of pinks and greens, blues and reds, and green, yellow and black were used. Domes and barrel-shaped ceilings were also popular with the Neo Classical designers. In the 19th century skylights of iron and glass created new lighting effects especially over stairwells, while a central flower or medallion moulding from which a chandelier was hung also became popular.

FIG 7.8: GREAT WITLEY CHURCH, WORCESTERSHIRE: *A section of stunning Rococo style ceiling which has been restored to its former glory in white and gilt at this church which stands alongside Witley Court.*

FIG 7.9: PANTHEON, ROME: *This vast domed building built by the Romans was visited by many British architects on their Grand Tours in the 18th century and subsequently inspired numerous room designs. You will recognise the square patterning of the dome in many houses and garden buildings today.*

▦ FLOORS

The original ground floors of a medieval house would have been of compounded earth. This was made by raking the surface, flooding it with water and then beating it with paddles when dry. Additives like lime, sand, bone chips, clay and bull's blood could also be used for strength or appearance. By the 16th and 17th century these rooms would be expected to be floored with stone slabs or perhaps the Dutch fashion of black and white marble tiles. Bricks and clay floor tiles were also common, with the earliest ones being generally larger and unglazed (glazed versions appear in the 18th century). Stone, brick and tiles were still used into the 20th century in service areas like the kitchen.

As basements became standard the ground floor above would usually, like the upper floors, be composed of floorboards. Early planks are wider, about one foot across, and were butted up against each other, with tongue and groove boarding only appearing in the 19th century. Stone and marble floors still featured in some grand rooms but obviously would require additional support in the basement below to hold the extra weight. Floor surfaces featuring marquetry and parquet wood patterns were popular in the early 18th century.

Carpets first appeared in the early 17th century and were laid even over the most elaborate floorings. In the late 18th century as one person increasingly controlled the interior design scheme, he would order a carpet from the manufacturer to be woven into a pattern to match his ceiling design.

In Victorian houses the wider range of architectural styles and greater specialisation of rooms results in broad range of surfaces, including contrasting stone or marble squares, mosaics, tongue and grooved floorboards and encaustic tiles (earthenware tiles onto which a pattern in different colours has been burnt into the surface). Plain, unglazed tiles in terracotta, black or buff were also popular in service rooms and areas of heavy use.

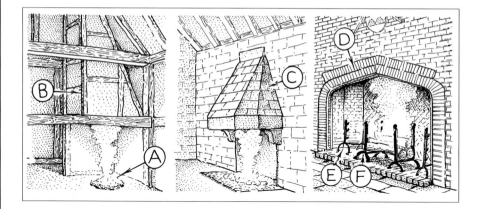

FIG 7.10: *Three interior views showing the development of the fireplace in the later Middle Ages. The left-hand view shows how the hearth (A) could be moved from its central position into a corner and a section between the supporting timbers panelled in with wood and daub to form a smoke bay (B) above it. Another possibility was a smoke hood (C) which could be made from masonry as in this case or from timber and daub, and tended to project out into the room by up to 5 ft. The final view shows a 16th century fireplace with the hearth now set in the wall and the recess crowned by a Tudor brick arch (D). This example also shows the cob irons (E) which supported the spits on which food was roasted in front of the fire, the logs of which were held in place by the firedogs (F).*

⌗ FIREPLACES

In the great medieval hall the smoke from the central fire escaped usually through a louvre (French for 'the opening') in the apex of the roof. In this time before matches, lighting a fire was a problem, so it was often left ablaze overnight with a pottery colander called a couvre-feu (French for a 'fire cover', from which we get the word curfew!) placed over it.

The first improvements came with a smoke screen which trapped the smoke from a hearth at one end of the room, then large hoods often made of timber and daub which hung over a fire along the wall, until finally the fireplace and chimney developed.

The surround or chimneypiece was typically a wide, flat-arched opening in Tudor houses, as this was what was required to contain a large log-burning fire. During the 16th century coal from the North East became available to the rich and later fireplaces are smaller as this new fuel needed less space in which to produce the same heat. Unfortunately for the men who used to climb up the chimney to clean it, these new types were too narrow, so from this period on boys were used!

By the late 16th century the fireplace had developed into a principal feature in a room and was lavishly decorated. In later Classical houses it fell from prominence, although its position in the centre of the wall enhanced the

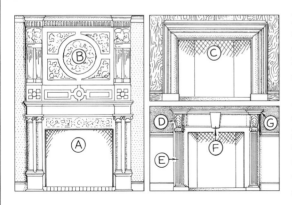

FIG 7.11: *The left-hand view shows a chimneypiece design typical of the late 16th and early 17th century. The lower section (A) is often seen as one with the upper half (B) in marble, plaster, stone or timber, and its dominant size and lavish decoration shows how it was a major feature in Elizabethan and Jacobean houses. The top right design is late 17th century and has what is known as a 'bolection' moulding running around the fireplace (C). To the bottom right is an 18th century example with classical decoration like scrolled brackets (D), pilasters (E) and a keystone (F). The mantel (G) along the top was still of a shallow depth at this date.*

FIG 7.12: *A late 18th century chimneypiece designed by Robert Adam. His examples are often distinguished by human figures in place of columns (called caryatids) at each side and by a plaque with a raised decorative scene in the middle. The mantel above tends to be deeper by this date. Rather than the firedogs which held logs in fig 7.10, the now smaller opening features a firegrate which holds coal in a compact block to increase combustion.*

FIG 7.13: *Later Victorian fireplaces often had the iron firegrate surrounded by decorative tiles.*

symmetry of the room. The surrounds of stone or marble were more refined and typically had a shallow shelf supported by columns or brackets. Later 18th century pieces had broader mantels and often featured sculptured figures supporting it, or the latest in Neo Classical motifs. The popular Adam's styled surrounds could also feature a central plaque decorated with interlocking foliage and scrolls. Improvements in design meant the 19th century fireplace could be even smaller, often with cast iron hearths and surrounds which Victorians would decorate with patterned tiles.

▨ DOORS

Early doors were typically vertical planks of wood fixed by nails to horizontal beams, and held onto the frame by iron hinges or pins. These and their variants may have sufficed in a Tudor manor but the Renaissance gentleman and his descendants demanded something to fit in with their classical decoration. Panelled doors thus developed, early ones with just two panels but by the 18th century the familiar six panel design was the most common. Not only were these doors elegant but they were also lighter, so smaller butt hinges, (that is, the type used on most doors today, with two rectangular plates held together by a pin), could be used which could be concealed out of sight between door and frame. Dark woods like mahogany and oak were left exposed, but if cheaper

FIG 7.14: OSTERLEY PARK, MIDDLESEX: *Double doors which together feature six panels, the lower two of which are flush with the frame for extra strength where the door was likely to take most wear and tear.*

softwoods like pine were used they would always be painted, this same rule applying to any other wood panelling or carving in the room.

The surrounds which had been modest Tudor arches or moulded and carved frames, after the Restoration became lavish door-cases embellished with columns and Baroque decoration with entablatures and a pediment across the top. Sometimes a set of double doors were fitted, usually to help keep food odours out of adjoining rooms, while the famous green baize door which separated the main house from the service rooms had the material pinned to one side to keep offensive noises from reaching the gentry.

✳ STAIRS

The earliest way of ascending to what few upper rooms there were in a medieval house was by a ladder, or in a more impressive stone building by a narrow spiral staircase. As rooms on upper floors gained importance, wider and more elaborate stairs were required to reach them, often contained in a projection at the rear or built within a tower.

By the early 17th century the more familiar framed newel staircase was becoming popular. This had the separate treads and risers, which made up the steps, held in place by a side string course which was supported on thick corner and end posts called newels (see fig 7.16). If the 16th century is the Age of the Chimney, then the 17th could be rightly called the Age of the Staircase. They were considered great status symbols and in the Jacobean period their oak posts and balusters were beautifully decorated, often displaying coats of arms with carvings of beasts or features from nature on top of the newels. Their

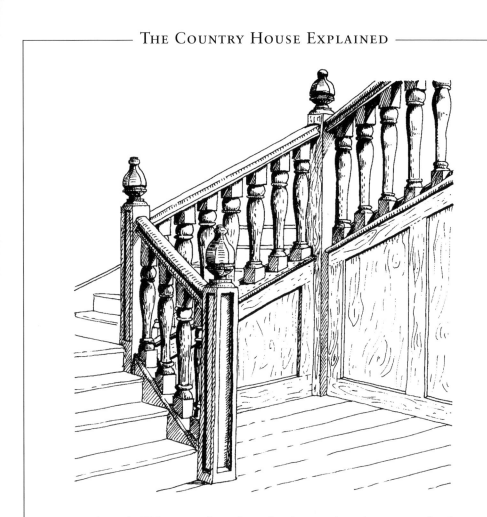

FIG 7.15: *An early 17th century framed newel staircase, where the corner and end posts rest directly on the floor with the space beneath panelled in.*

importance could be further emphasised by being built in a separate room, often at the end of the hall, with their steps and landings wrapping around all four sides. A few examples still have carved dog gates at the bottom, which were used to keep the animals in the hall at night.

As joinery techniques improved the newel posts ceased to rest on the floor, and the steps appeared to float upwards, although they were actually cantilevered off the wall. Some staircases had their now exposed undersides plastered like a ceiling with decorative mouldings and even pictures, while others had beautiful marquetry or parquet floors fitted on the landings and elaborate carved posts. By the late 17th century the balusters had become more elegant and numerous and in the grandest houses there were even some made from wrought iron, combined with wooden rails and marble steps.

While the important rooms of state remained on the first floor then impressive staircases at the end of the hall or even rising up from within the room itself were still built. Baroque houses though tended to have their state withdrawing rooms and bedchambers arranged along the rear of the ground floor (the enfilade), so their guests did not need to go upstairs and thus the staircase became less prominent. In the 18th century Palladian houses these important rooms for parading were on the raised piano nobile which was accessed by the stone steps at the front of the house, under the portico.

In many houses, especially in 16th and 17th century buildings that were being updated, the staircase remained important and by the Regency period decorated ironwork balusters with mahogany rails ending in elegant curves were all the rage. Victorian staircases are dependent upon the style of house,

---

FIG 7.16: *The left-hand staircase is another Jacobean example with elaborate wood carving. The steps are composed of risers (A) and treads (B), held in place by the newel posts (C), balusters (D), and the string course (E). The gate (F) remains in a few houses and was closed at night to keep the dogs downstairs. The top right design (G) is 18th century, by which time the balusters have become thinner and the stairs are supported off the wall so the underside is open. Barleytwist balusters and having two or three per tread were common features. The bottom right staircase (H) is a late 18th century type by Robert Adam who preferred to use simple iron balusters as in this example.*

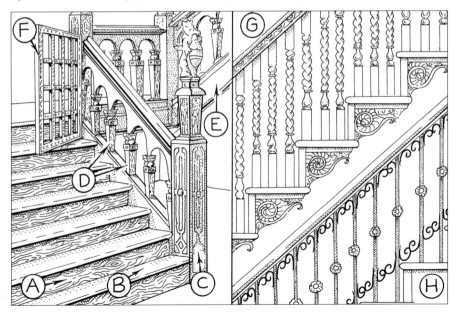

although despite the availability of iron, bulky wooden balusters reappear in many houses. With guests' bedrooms now back upstairs they become prominent once again, although there is a general shift to more simple styling.

FIG 7.17: *A later Georgian staircase with a semi-circular extension to the bottom tread and above it a coiled end to the wooden rail which crowns the iron balusters. Where the treads extend out over the string course as in this example it is referred to as an 'open string' and this was popular during the 18th century. A 'closed string' where the treads run into the inside of the string course (fig 7.15) was typical of early stair design but was featured again in the later houses of those revival-obsessed Victorians.*

CHAPTER 8

The Principal Rooms

As previously mentioned, the selection, size and arrangement of rooms in the country house reflect the personal demands and expectations of the owner, his family and his guests. No one house is the same as another. There were, however, certain fashionable room types although the date at which they appear can vary greatly, as with all parts of the house, depending on how close the property was to major cities and the owner to court and political life. This chapter will look at the most common room types, the general dates at which they were popular and features to look out for within.

It is worth noting though that despite these periodic changes the rooms on

FIG 8.1: WEALD AND DOWNLAND OPEN AIR MUSEUM, SUSSEX: *Two views of the same hall, as it may have appeared in this smaller 15th century country house, stripped bare of decoration and most furniture. The left-hand view is looking towards the service end with the two openings in the middle giving entrance to the buttery and pantry while the door in the right corner is opposite another on the left; in later houses these have a screened passage running between them. The right-hand view is looking towards the lord's end of the hall with doors through to his private chambers. Note the large window with shutters and the central hearth in the foreground, which has blackened the roof timbers above.*

FIG 8.2: *A view of a late medieval hall with elaborate window openings and straw covering the floor. The dais (A) has upon it the lord's seat with its canopy (B) to keep out the chills and a large oriel window (C) illuminating this end of the room. Above are the trusses (D) supporting the roof timbers, while in the middle is the central hearth (E). At the entrance end of the hall is the screen (F) the inserting of which has formed a minstrels' gallery above (G) and a passage below (H). The earliest screens were free-standing and portable (I), while later fixed ones featured beautiful carving (J).*

show in many houses today will have been laid out in the 19th and early 20th century and often seem like a procession of similar, lavishly decorated voids. Although some bodies like the National Trust have endeavoured to return interiors to earlier periods in the history of a house, the original use of the room may only be discernible from its size, position within the layout or the detailing in its decoration.

▓ The Hall

Whether it was a medieval knight stepping through the timber doorway into his lord's manor house or a Georgian gentleman entering a fellow aristocrat's mansion from under a towering portico, their first impression of their host's power or refinement would be cast by the hall. Yet this room was originally much more than somewhere to take off your coat, more than just a vestibule full of sculptures and portraits, in fact it started its life as the very house itself.

The Saxon or Norman manor house would usually have consisted of one large building, very much like a barn, surrounded by lesser structures and an external fence or wall (see chapter 1). This principal building was the hall. The lord, his fellow nobles, personal army, and servants would eat, drink and sleep in this one cavernous space. In the middle was a hearth with the fumes from the fire drifting up through blackened timbers and a gap in the roof, while at

FIG 8.3: WOLLATON HALL, NOTTINGHAMSHIRE: *The hall of this Elizabethan prodigy house which was partly inspired by castles, still contains medieval style features like the decorated timber roof trusses, in this case with coats of arms, a screens passage with the two door openings and the minstrels' gallery above (note the top of the doorways at each end of it).*

belching servants, snoring soldiers and scratching dogs, upon filthy and muck ridden straw, somehow lost its appeal for later medieval lords! They built wings and extensions onto their halls to create private rooms in what is called the solar. At the other end a buttery and pantry were added, often with a passage between to access the separate kitchen. The later Middle Ages were also a time of great social changes accelerated by the Black Death, which saw the breaking down of the old feudal system and the renting out of manor lands. Decisions on managing the fields were increasingly made by the new yeoman farmers and therefore the hall's role as the centre of the estate and community faded. By the 15th and 16th centuries the hearths were being removed to the sides, ceilings inserted and rooms created above. Note though that these changes to the running of the estate occurred at different times across the country, and the hall may have still been fulfilling its communal role in some areas at a later date.

Those genuine medieval halls which survive today usually have the whitewash and paintwork stripped from their walls, stone slabs on the floor where straw and earth sufficed and glass in windows where once oiled cloth or shutters kept out the cold. Despite this it would be difficult not to be impressed by the scale of the room and the impressive timber trusses which support the roof above. Another area where the carver could show off his skill with wood was on the screen. Keeping warm was a major problem in such a large room, so to reduce the draughts which would come howling through the main doorway a screen was built, at first a movable one but later fixed, which created a passage at one end of the hall (screens passage). By the 16th century

one end was a raised platform, the dais, from which the lord dealt justice, gathered men in arms, managed his farmland and was entertained. The hall was a bedroom, dining room, a theatre and a courtroom. It was the centre of the community and all were welcome.

However, sleeping with a group of

these screens had become elaborately carved, often with a platform above from which minstrels could play. A popular piece of decoration in the medieval hall was the lord's coat of arms, which not only represented his high status but also, when formed into a family tree of arms (often in the stained glass of oriel windows, see fig 1.5), displayed his links to important or powerful families.

At the same time as many peasants were still enjoying the hospitality of their lord, Renaissance aristocrats and gentlemen were erecting new houses for display, with a series of refined, classically decorated rooms with which to impress their guests. The hall was often still the centre of the house and placed lengthways across it when viewed from the front. For the first time though at Hardwick Hall it was turned 90° (see fig 2.10) and became the long, thin entrance room we associate it with today. As the hall was now one of the rooms through which guests passed, you would hardly want servants eating and sleeping within, so gradually separate accommodation and a servants' hall in which they could

FIG 8.4: KEDLESTON HALL, DERBYSHIRE: *In the 18th century fantastic marble and stone halls were a feature of Palladian houses. This example by Robert Adam has columns made from local alabaster (a form of gypsum or limestone) with flutings which were cut on site, arched niches containing sculptures and a huge coffered ceiling above.*

take meals were created.

The 17th century hall would usually be wood panelled with a new patterned plaster ceiling. It would have within it, or off to one end, a beautifully carved staircase by which guests could ascend to the state rooms. By the 18th century it had risen in importance again, forming part of the piano nobile on the first floor with usually external steps leading up to it. The vivid colours which were popular in Palladian houses, to best display gilt-framed pictures, gradually made way for pale, plastered walls with columns and a floor of light coloured stone and marble. These cool rooms could also be used for dining in the heat of summer as well as being spacious enough to welcome a party of guests or to serve as an antechamber. Later, the assortment of styles available to the Victorian gentleman resulted in halls of medieval grandeur in mock Tudor houses, as well as ones that were more of an extended stairwell with illumination from above.

FIG 8.5: AVONCROFT MUSEUM OF HISTORIC BUILDINGS, WORCESTERSHIRE: *The upper chamber or solar of a medieval house with the hall down below reached through the opening to the left.*

▨ THE GREAT CHAMBER

One of the first rooms to appear when the owner sought more privacy from his medieval hall was an upper chamber in which he could dine and sleep called the solar (from the Latin word *solarium*, with the root *sol*, meaning sun). Food was brought up in a procession from the service rooms at the other end of the hall, past his household sitting along tables in the hall and then up a staircase at the side of the dais. By the later Middle Ages though, the lord was likely to be receiving guests in the solar and eating in state so with its increased status the room became more lavishly decorated and had a separate bedchamber leading off it. Around this time it became known as the great chamber.

The great chamber was popular during the 16th and early 17th century and it could usually be found upstairs in a crosswing or built directly above the hall when this was divided horizontally by inserting a ceiling. Displaying hanging tapestries or family portraits, it was used for important meals and sometimes for music, plays and dancing. Wood panelling was added to the walls and the chairs would have had horsehair covers (which did not retain the smell of food). Details like royal coats of arms above the chimneypiece and hunting themes in the decoration were popular. Later chambers started to increase in scale with coved ceilings while paintings were built in above the chimneypiece and carved features such as fruit, flowers and birds adorned the panelling.

FIG 8.6: CALKE ABBEY, DERBYSHIRE: *The dining room created in 1794 is decorated with plaster mouldings framing small inset pictures, while the alcove behind the columns features a sideboard which could be used when serving meals. Note the door just behind the right-hand column which could give servants discreet access to the room.*

❈ THE BANQUETING HALL

In the later medieval hall, once the dignitaries had finished their main course they could retire to a separate room to eat a luxurious selection of wafers and spices. In the 16th century this was also referred to as a 'banquet' (and not just the huge meal which we associate with the word), and in some larger houses an impressive room was constructed specifically for it. The banqueting hall often had access to the roof, or in some cases was even built on top of it so the relaxing diners could admire the views. Whole banqueting houses were sometimes built as separate structures out in the garden.

❈ THE PARLOUR

Such a large room was excessive for everyday meals, so a parlour would have been provided for the family. Parlour comes from the French verb *parler*, to speak, and it could have also been a room in which to hold private conversation. They can be found in country houses from the 15th century and were usually simply decorated with an oval gateleg table which could be removed when required. There was little other furniture as masses of plates and cutlery were not used at this time; the guest brought their own knife and spoon, and forks were not in general use until the 18th century. Larger houses may have had more than one, perhaps a great and little parlour, while in 18th and 19th century houses you will probably find a selection of rooms intended for the family to dine in, often labelled by the certain times of the day or season in which they were used (for example, 'breakfast room').

THE DINING ROOM

By the 18th century a new room within the state apartments on the piano nobile began to appear. The dining room replaced the great chamber as the place where important meals were held, becoming a major element in 19th country houses where it was as much for show as for eating. Walls were usually plastered or stuccoed with floral, fruit and animal designs around the cornice and friezes while shutters were recommended in place of curtains to avoid lingering food odours.

Victorians were better at ergonomics than their predecessors and would rather receive their meals hot, so the dining room would not be positioned too far from the kitchen. A serving area would be nearby where the different parts of the meal were collected before they were brought into the room. Some even had hidden doorways so that servants could emerge to remove dishes with minimal fuss. It was only in the 19th century that the table became a fixed piece of furniture in the middle of what was now a permanent dining room, rather than the previous gateleg type which could be removed and the chairs pushed up against the walls when the room was to be used for another purpose.

THE SALOON

The great chamber died out from the late 17th century, its role being taken over by the dining room and saloon in the state apartments of Baroque and Palladian houses. The saloon (a French word

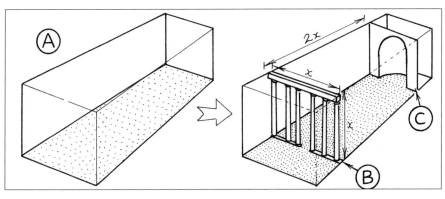

FIG 8.7: *State rooms like the hall, saloon and dining rooms of new 18th century country houses would preferably form a single or double cube. When refitting an existing house, however, moving walls to create these proportions was not usually practical. At Syon House, London, Robert Adam was faced with a long thin room (A), so he ingeniously inserted a screen of columns (B) and an apse (C), thus making the space between them a double cube.*

FIG 8.8: WOLLATON HALL, NOTTINGHAMSHIRE: *By the Victorian period the tables and chairs could be scattered around the room as in this example rather than left up against the wall.*

derived from the Italian *sala*, meaning a hall) was ideally placed centrally, behind the entrance hall, with the dining room and drawing room on each side and views over the garden to the rear. This room was regarded as essential in 18th century houses and would be as tall as the hall, even if this meant lifting the floor of the room above. Architects could make use of its grand scale and produced domed round rooms or large double cubed spaces with alcoves and apses, with huge coffered ceilings and shallow bowed windows.

It was here that the best pieces of artwork, sculpture and furniture could be displayed, and concerts, balls and other entertainment held. As the room was not used for dining, the walls could be covered in delicate fabrics and paintings hung upon them. By the 19th century many saloons had become no more than picture galleries, and were referred to as such, with glass panels in the ceiling, very much like a Victorian museum, while dances and great gatherings could take place in a separate ballroom.

WITHDRAWING ROOMS

As the medieval solar developed into the more luxurious great chamber, a separate bedroom was usually built off it for the owner. Between these rooms an antechamber was supplied where he could take a private meal in the days before a parlour, and his servant could sleep on a straw pallet and guard the door to his bedroom. This room was referred to as the withdrawing room.

By the late 16th and early 17th century the room had become more of a private sitting room where the owner could hang his favourite or best pieces of art. In Baroque houses though it formed part of the state apartments and was nearly always positioned between the saloon and the bedchambers. In 18th century houses it was still expected to be an intimate room, often with a lower ceiling than the saloon and hall, delicate fabrics on the walls and curtains with pelmets around the windows (before it became fashionable to hang them in all rooms). It was regarded as a feminine room; while the men stayed on to smoke and drink in the dining room, the ladies would retire to what was now generally referred to as the drawing room. Its role was vague – you could find card tables, spinning wheels or a piano within, music often being the decorative theme. Through the Regency period the informality grew with chairs in groups around the room rather than up against the walls; the French fashion for hanging a mirror above the fireplace became popular and there was increased comfort and luxury with large draped pelmets gathered above the curtains. Today, the drawing room has become a place with no specific purpose and rooms where their original role has been forgotten are often labelled as such.

▦ BEDCHAMBERS

The most recognised symbol of a country house bedroom is the four poster bed. They became common by the 16th century, giving the occupants a form of draught exclusion and some much needed privacy in bedrooms, which even

when separated from the old great chambers still had a medley of servants buzzing around through the day. Four posters became the single most expensive item of furniture in a house and were usually positioned on the opposite side of the room from the windows which had a dressing table and looking glass on the wall between them. By the late 17th century a separate room for dressing was provided so the table became more of a showpiece.

In the Baroque houses of this date the state bedchamber was at the end of the enfilade after the saloon and withdrawing rooms, although it was less ornate than those which preceded it. In late 17th and early 18th century bedchambers there was a fashion for positioning the four poster behind rails or within an alcove divided off from the rest of the room by columns. This helped keep the room clear for other uses through the day, and made a grand climax to the procession of retiring to the state bed, although there may have also been a door to the side of the alcove for the occupant to access another more private bed after the ceremony.

With the end of the piano nobile in the 19th century and the resiting of the principal rooms on the ground floor, the bedrooms went upstairs, although it was usual to retain a bedchamber on the ground floor for infirm or elderly members of the family. These new rooms tended to be smaller than the old state bedchambers but more numerous as the Victorian gentleman was likely to be entertaining large parties of guests rather than smaller family groups.

Going back to the late 17th century, additional rooms off the bedchamber were being provided for dressing, where possible at the far end of the enfilade. In the case of a lady there was a dressing room, while the gentleman's version was known as a cabinet. William III met his closest circle of ministers within his cabinet and the name still refers to the group of senior ministers in government today. Corner fireplaces and oriental artwork were popular and small pictures were often hung here as these rooms tended to have lower ceilings than the bedroom. This meant that a space above could be provided for the servants. By the later 18th century ladies were likely to have a boudoir (from the French word *bouder*, meaning sulk!), a private sitting room where they could sew or read in increasing luxury. As bedchambers moved upstairs and became the conventional bedroom the male cabinets next to them were known simply as dressing rooms.

Another room off the bedchamber or dressing room was the closet, a room for keeping the close stool (basically a chamber pot covered by a closed top with a hole in it). In earlier medieval houses a chamber pot would have been used in the great chamber while separate garderobes may have been provided elsewhere. These were tiny rooms with a simple hole in a board to form a toilet seat and either earth below which could afterwards be used as fertilizer, or a drop down directly into the moat. In 16th century country houses the closet may have been no more than a cupboard sized room with no light or ventilation. This was bad enough for the dignitary who had to use it, even worse for the poor servant who had to walk through the house with a pot full of effluent afterwards! By the later 17th century the closet had become more of a private sanctuary, a larger room where the owner could expect to be seated on something more luxurious, like veneered wood or even a velvet seat, while his waste would be carried away with more privacy. The invention of flushing toilets and bathrooms in the 19th century made closets a thing of the past.

FIG 8.9: *A bedchamber with a rail closing off the alcove containing the four poster bed, with a doorway to the left of it giving access to a private sleeping room. These rails were only a short-lived fashion and rarely survive today although the bed may still be found in an alcove.*

FIG 8.10: LITTLE MORETON HALL, CHESHIRE: *The left-hand photograph shows the garderobe extension which protrudes from the front of the building. The right-hand picture shows the interior of one of the garderobes with the toilet seat hole leading directly down into the moat which runs below.*

▥ The Long Gallery

Today's glass-roofed leisure parks are not the bright new idea they might appear. Elizabethans were well aware of the limitations of the English weather and built themselves huge long rooms for recreational use, illuminated by masses of glass windows. These long galleries were in high fashion for a relatively short period from the mid 16th to mid 17th century, yet their distinctive long, thin form are a notable feature of numerous country houses even after later alterations. They can be more than 170 ft in length, have at least two walls full of glass, with wood panelling elsewhere, so the family and their guests could admire the view while promenading along the boarded floor. The rooms were used for sports like real tennis, games including billiards or shove halfpenny on long shuffleboards, and even work outs on early dumb bells or exercise chairs! Others were more educational with portraits of important dignitaries lining one of the walls and symbols with hidden meanings in the plasterwork. They were a gym, sports hall, art gallery and viewing tower all in one.

FIG 8.11: LITTLE MORETON HALL, CHESHIRE: *The spectacular Long Gallery is perched on top of this characteristically contorted timber framed house (see fig 1.1). Horizontal beams and rods in the ceiling help hold the structure together, but all in all its uneven and twisted form remains surprisingly secure. Real tennis was probably played here as two early 17th century balls were discovered behind the panelling, although as the game required a space more like a squash court some type of shutters may have been hung over the windows!*

Their shape, however, did not fit easily into the later Baroque houses and although some were built in the 18th century for artwork, dances and after dinner chats, many of the existing ones became libraries or picture galleries. By the Victorian period their role, as was usual, had been absorbed by numerous smaller rooms, with the children now playing in the nursery, male recreation taking place in the billiards room, the ladies using their boudoir or drawing room, topical discussions being held in the study and dancing in the ballroom.

▨ LIBRARY

The 17th century gentleman who collected curiosities usually stored them in his cabinet (off the bedchamber) but the 18th century connoisseur who bought up much larger works of art, sculpture and literature would have to find more room. The spacious Palladian halls, saloons, drawing rooms and dining rooms would house his artworks, but a separate library would now be required for his books.

At this time collecting books was a new fashion inspired by an intellectual thirst for Art and Politics, but in medieval or Tudor households they were rarely found, not only because few were made but also because prowess on the field of arms was more important than gaining knowledge. The Renaissance man educated in the Humanities may have started gathering some volumes but these precious items would not be kept in one particular place. In the 17th century, especially after the founding of scientific societies, more books were likely to be collected and were usually stored in the gentlemen's closet (keeping a book or newspaper in the toilet today is not such a new idea). In fact early libraries, which at the time were very much male preserves, can often be found built off the closet.

By the 18th century though, the importance of literature had elevated the library to a state room, increasingly used by all the family as a place for letter writing, playing cards or as a meeting place for guests. Open bookcases became popular from the mid 1700s, replacing earlier glass cabinets, while the awakening of interest in English history and literature later in the century inspired a fashion of Gothic styled libraries.

▨ CHAPEL

The importance of religion in daily life in medieval England meant that it would be unthinkable not to have a chapel or church, and usually both, at hand for the lord and his household. The private chapel was used for daily prayers while the parish church next door would be attended by the owner, his family and household along with the parish every Sunday. In larger houses the chapel would usually have a comfortable gallery above for the lord and his family, which could be accessed from their private apartments, while the household could use the main body of the room below.

Chapels that survive today are often in the earliest part of a house, as very few were built after the Reformation of the 1530s, although many had a later flamboyant Baroque or cool Classical refit. These impressively decorated chapels were often partly a show of anti Catholic feeling, but when this religious fever of the 1600s died down in the following century there was a lack of interest in chapel and church building generally.

However, the situation was very different for the suppressed Catholics. Ever since the Reformation there had been a constant battle between the Catholics who pledged allegiance to the Pope and those who protested against him, the Protestants. England was not a powerful country in the 16th century, so when the Catholic Mary, Queen of Scots was executed in 1587 and Catholic Spain dispatched the Armada for revenge, there was great fear in the country. This fuelled a witch hunt with the express intention of destroying Popery. Legislation for the conviction of Catholics and to reward those who betrayed them was set in place.

It was from this date and into the 17th century that priest holes were built in the homes of practising Catholics. Their sons were sent abroad to become priests and then returned as secret missionaries, often basing themselves at remote homes of staunch supporters and from here visiting local Catholics. Ingenious hiding places were thus required in which they could secrete themselves when the dreaded Pursuivants (priest hunters) came knocking. Many timber framed and stone Tudor mansions have more than one hidden passage or secret chamber still to be found today.

As previously mentioned though, this religious fever calmed down in the 1700s and by the latter part of the century Catholics were permitted to have a chapel, perhaps just a converted room, although it was not allowed to be visible as such from the outside. It was not until the Catholic Emancipation Act of 1829 that they could once again build new chapels and churches.

FIG 8.12: BADDESLEY CLINTON, WARWICKSHIRE: *The sacristy, a room off the chapel where the vestments and sacred vessels were stored, has an innocent looking box with a cross upon it on the far wall. This, however, covers a secret passage leading to a priest hole which was used when the house was raided in 1591. The Catholic fugitives may have hesitated, though, if they had realised that the hole they were dropping down was previously the garderobe shaft!*

CHAPTER 9

The Service Rooms

It was one thing to excite guests with architectural magnificence and lavish decoration, but the country house owner would also have to satisfy their stomachs in order to leave them with a positive impression of his or her hospitality. Medieval lords are known to have spent anything from half to three-quarters of their entire income on food and drink, and even in Victorian mansions vast sums went on maintaining specialist staff and buildings in order to create an almost self sufficient conveyor belt of meals. The fittings and layout of most service rooms that survive in country houses today date from this latter period.

The status and mix of people who manned these rooms changed over the centuries and the strict hierarchical structure of discreet, black and white dressed servants who would never speak directly to their employer is a rather late development and far removed from earlier arrangements. As already mentioned, the medieval country house was not designed for external show but rather in line with internal function and its household was a community composed from some of almost the same status as the lord himself down to local peasants from the area he was visiting. They would eat and drink with him in his hall, fight with him in his battles and expect a certain degree of protection in return for their service.

The move by the owner of the house from the 14th and 15th century towards more privacy gradually broke up this communal household. By the 17th century there was less emphasis on military skills for young aristocrats and they were no longer sent into a lord's service. At the same time, the lesser gentry set up their own households with a smaller number of staff. These servants were now of a lower, uniform status in a world of widening social division. They were expected to keep out of sight and were increasingly female although at first women were involved mainly in the preparation of food. It wasn't until the Victorian and Edwardian times that the structure of servants strictly adhering to rules and regulations, which we are familiar with from period dramas, reached its zenith. These servants now worked in a wider range of specialist rooms covering all aspects of food storage, production, cooking and serving, as well as the cleaning of utensils, linen and clothes. Fig 9.1 shows how these rooms could be arranged around a kitchen courtyard, with the arrows showing the route that food and drinks took from production to finally appearing as a meal in the dining room. This chapter looks at the role of these rooms and the features you may find in them today.

❖ THE KITCHEN

The most important room around which most of the other service rooms were arranged was the kitchen. Its internal arrangement and position within the confines of the country house were mainly dependent on a constant battle

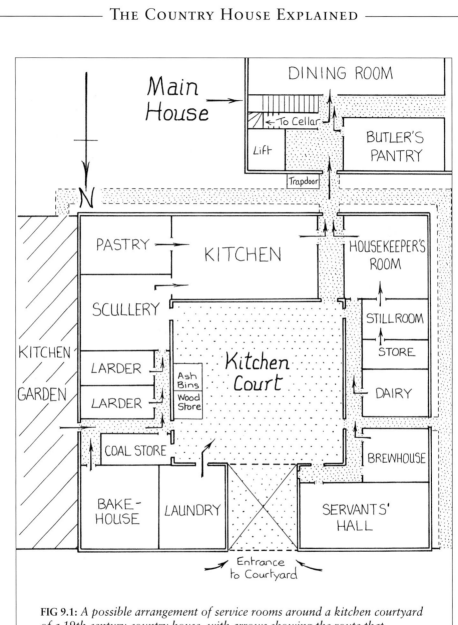

FIG 9.1: *A possible arrangement of service rooms around a kitchen courtyard of a 19th century country house, with arrows showing the route that ingredients, food and then the finished meals took to reach the dining room. The Victorians were the first to plan the layout of the service rooms with a real understanding of ergonomics.*

FIG 9.2: STANTON HARCOURT MANOR, OXFORDSHIRE: *External and internal shots of one of the few remaining medieval kitchens in the country. The left-hand photograph shows the square stone structure with a blocked up arch in the bottom right through which meals were passed into a covered passage (a pentise) leading to the hall and parlours. The dark area just below the pointed roof was originally a louvre filled with movable horizontal slats which could be adjusted to let the smoke out depending on wind direction. In the bottom left of the internal photograph you can see the doorway through which children passed on their way to the battlements at the top, to make the adjustments to the louvre – which is today filled with glass. The other three arched openings were baking ovens (see fig 9.10), while the main fire which was used primarily for roasting was up against the opposing wall. There was also a well in the middle of the floor to supply fresh water (similar to the one in fig 1.2) as the moat and other surface water around the medieval house were likely to be contaminated with waste.*

for fire safety and the removal of the odours produced in cooking. It was a smelly, noisy and dangerous place and not every lord therefore wanted it right next to his dining room!

The earliest kitchens in medieval houses, of which a few survive today, were constructed as separate buildings, timber framed or stone structures, often square in plan with pointed roofs and a louvre opening at the top. This was principally to reduce the fire risk to the main hall if the kitchen went up in flames, although there was the age old problem of the food becoming cold as it was transported. This was done in a procession, along a covered way, into the house via the kitchen passage, along the hall and into the lord's private chamber beyond. It is likely though that much of the cooking was still done on the hearth in the hall or on a stone or cobbled area outside the kitchen.

By the Tudor period the kitchen was usually part of the main house, typically one of the rooms around the courtyard or clustered with other service rooms on the other side of the passage from the hall

FIG 9.3: *An imaginary 16th or 17th century kitchen. The fire (A) held within the metal firedogs cooks the food supported on cob irons (B) and the spit (C). A clockwork mechanism spins the wheel (D) at the end of the spit though at this date most were probably turned by young boys. The fat dripping from the joints is caught in a tray below (E), other food is heated in pots hanging from the rail (F) and spare spits are stored above the fire (G). In the corner is a baking oven (H) with the peels (flat wooden shovels) used to insert and extract the bread leaning against the wall.*

An important feature which rarely survives today was the stove (I); most were replaced by ranges in the 19th century. Fuel was stored in the recesses below (J) while the gaps (K) above allowed air in to feed the charcoals held on round gridirons above (like a barbecue today). Pots were held above the heat on metal trivets or from a crane (L), allowing the food to be cooked gently. A feature of most country house kitchens which appears in all periods is the large central table (M) on which the meals were prepared.

FIG 9.4: *A Victorian kitchen with a closed range built into an old fireplace on the left and an open range retained on the far wall, with a spit in front turned by a smoke jack (see fig 9.5). Note the tall ceiling with windows and vents, dressers storing the massive selection of pots, pans, utensils and moulds, and in the middle the table with slatted boards for the cooks to stand upon.*

(see the stippled areas on the house plans in fig 2.10). Walls might be lime-washed plaster, with floors of stone or brick covered in straw or rushes. Cooking would be done on spits in front of a hearth set in a wide fireplace (see fig 7.10D), while there would be baking ovens with arched openings built into the wall and a charcoal stove on which delicate dishes like sauces could be simmered. There may have also been a separate boiling house with a large copper in which stews, stock and meats could be cooked. Although there would be a table for preparation other furniture was limited as there were fewer cooking utensils and implements to store.

In the 17th century the division that was opened up between the elite and service sides of the country house saw the kitchen increasingly moved into the basement to keep the servants out of sight

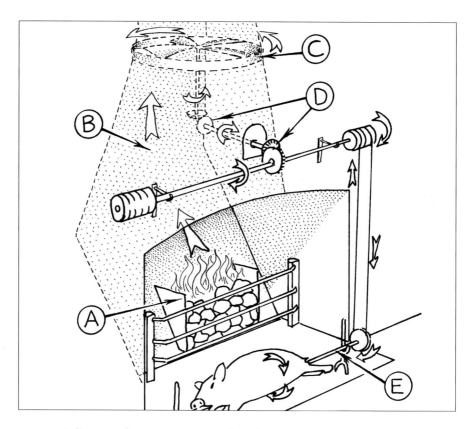

FIG 9.5: *A diagram of a roasting range and smoke jack. The sides (A) of the range were adjustable and controlled the size of the fire. The spit in front of it was turned by the smoke jack which was powered by smoke rising up the flue (B) spinning the fan (C) above, and turning the connecting shafts and gears (D) which, via a horizontal rod above the fireplace and a pulley at the end, spun the spit (E) below.*

of the family and guests above. Some had stone vaulted ceilings which helped reduce the fire risk, while ranges, raised iron firebaskets which held the increasingly available coal rather than wood, were popular. In later Palladian houses the kitchen was on the move again, this time out of the way in a separate pavilion or wing (see figs 4.9 and 4.11), although many of the male dominated areas like the butlers' and stewards' rooms and the precious beer and wine cellars remained below the main house. In the pavilion the kitchen could be two storeys high with other single storey service rooms around it and servants' bedchambers above them. Some still had large hearths, but most featured ever more elaborate roasting ranges with mechanical spits and hob areas to the

FIG 9.6: COGGES MANOR FARM MUSEUM, OXFORDSHIRE: *From the 1780s improvements were made to the range, with an iron baking oven to one side and a boiler on the other while the fire between them still had cooking pots and kettles suspended by a crane or on trivets. In the first half of the 19th century, though, more efficient closed ranges appeared in which the central fire had an iron plate above it and the hot fumes were forced out around the ovens on either side rather than wasted straight up the chimney. Circular hobs on top of the range gave a gentle heat for simmering, thus removing the need for a separate stove, or could have the iron centre part removed to give a more intense heat. A boiler was built in behind the fire and a rack above could be used for plate warming. The example in this photograph was designed in the 1890s and although it was versatile it required blacking every day, constant adjustment of dampers to control the heat, and extra ventilation had to be provided now the chimney above was enclosed.*

sides. Walls were sometimes painted blue as the colour was believed to repel flies.

The huge kitchens with masses of strange and elaborate devices which feature on country house tours today are usually a product of the later 19th century. In the early Victorian period it became difficult to retain staff as many villagers went off to work in the factories, so the Lady of the House became increasingly involved in the running of the kitchen. This prompted them to improve the standards below the stairs or, as in many new houses of the time, build better designed service courtyards to the rear or side of the house (see fig 5.26). New cast iron ranges, running water,

better ventilation and numerous time saving gadgets were designed to make life easier and more hygienic.

Walls were still lime-washed, white or yellow, while by the early 20th century glazed rectangular white wall tiles covered areas behind the sink and range and sometimes all around the room with virtually no grout between them, so as not to attract dirt and grease. The room was often tall with windows high up or in the ceiling with rods to open them and ventilate the room. Dressers stored the now massive assortment of utensils and pans, the *batterie de cuisine*. The Victorians loved jellies and numerous strangely shaped moulds for them are

FIG 9.7: *(A) shows a bain marie, a shallow sink filled with hot water designed to cook sauces or keep them warm. The copper pots within had tags on the handles to identify the contents. (B) is a warming trolley with metal lined doors and iron racks within. It was wheeled in front of the fire and the doors were opened, heating the crockery within and at the same time protecting the servants working behind from the immense heat that ranges emitted.*

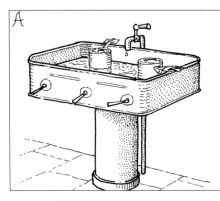

often found upon dressers. New technologies start to appear in the kitchen like steam cooking with boilers supplying pressurised steam to kettles containing food or to separate warming cupboards. The centre of the kitchen would be dominated by a large wooden table usually made of deal, for preparing the meals, with slatted boards around for servants to stand upon.

FIG 9.8: COGGES MANOR FARM MUSEUM, OXFORDSHIRE: *In addition to the range a freestanding roaster like the one in this photograph could be stood in front of the fire. A clockwork mechanism at the top would have turned the circular rack (which when in use would have been higher than shown here) from which the meat was hung. The heat from the fire would have reflected from the curved back onto the meat while the fat would have collected in the tray at the bottom.*

FIG 9.9: COGGES MANOR FARM MUSEUM: *A 19th century knife polisher. Abrasive powder was poured in through a hole at the top, the knives were inserted into the slots next to it and when the handle turned it rotated felt pads which with the powder polished the blades within.*

FIG 9.10: *The beehive shaped oven was first filled with wood, coal or a local fuel and heated up to temperature. The charcoal or ash was then removed and the bread put inside before the door was sealed for baking.*

FIG 9.11: *The iron door and opening of a brick oven which could be found not only in a bakehouse but also in other rooms like the kitchen, scullery, pastry and stillroom.*

▒ BAKEHOUSE

In larger houses separate rooms were provided for some types of cooking or preparation, and one was the bakehouse where bread, cakes and biscuits were produced. It was ideally in a separate block or at least as far from the house as possible so that the flour dust and oven odours would not penetrate indoors, and so deliveries of food stuffs and fuel were easier. The earliest ovens were brick beehive shaped with a small arched opening and may have taken a number of days to reach the correct temperature! (see fig 9.10). They proved better at baking, though, than the cast iron ovens that were introduced with 19th century ranges, and many survived into the 20th century. The room would also contain floorchests, benches with a trough for kneading the dough, and a sink for washing utensils like the peel, which was the wooden paddle used to lift the bread in and out of the oven.

▒ PASTRY

A few larger houses had a pastry which originally was where meat pies and pastries were made, although by the 19th century it was used for the production of confectionery, sweets and tarts. They are often found on the cool northern side of the service block, with the oven in an adjoining room. The room would contain shelves and pin racks, benches with marble tops for rolling pastry, and bins below for flour.

▒ STILLROOM

The name comes from its original role as where the 'stills' were kept for the production of perfumes, medicines, and cordial waters from flowers, herbs and spices. These usually separate stillhouses (due to the fire risk from the furnace used in the distilling process) were important in medieval and Tudor households and were usually run by the Lady of the House.

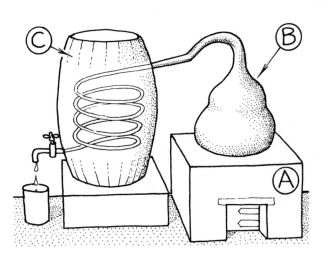

FIG 9.12: *A diagram showing 19th century distilling equipment which could be used to produce cordial waters. The furnace (A) heated up a mix of flower petals or herbs covered in liquid within the bottom of the still (B). The steam rose up and along the thin tube, condensing in the spiral within the worm tub (C) which was full of cold water.*

By the late 17th century the stillhouses were replaced by stillrooms in the new basements, and as the aristocracy would now never be seen there, the housekeeper took charge of the process and the still is often located next to her room. Polishes, waxes and soaps could be produced here but these, along with distilling, died out during the 18th century as it became easier to buy the products. By the 19th century the stillroom was mainly used for making preserves, pickles and desserts, for storing ingredients and for preparing light meals.

▦ DAIRY

The dairy was rare among the service rooms in that it could be lavishly designed and decorated. This was originally due to the involvement of the Lady of the House who up until the 19th century could often be found running its production of unadulterated milk, butter, cheese etc. Although it was usually part of the suite of service rooms it could also be a freestanding building or part of the estate farm, and to keep everything cool it would be preferable on the north or shaded side of the building.

FIG 9.13: *A view showing how hygienic and yet ornamental some dairies had become by the late 18th and early 19th century. The fountain in the middle emitted a spray to help keep the temperature down, while skimming dishes, pans, vases and churns stand upon the low stone table around the perimeter.*

FIG 9.14: *One of the types of churn to be found in a dairy for turning cream into butter. A plunge churn had a vertical barrel with a plunger on top, while an up and over churn had the barrel spun on the opposite axis to the one shown here.*

By the late 18th century the Gentleman of the House became interested in all forms of agricultural improvement and the application of science to farm production, including the dairy. The rooms they built had white tiled walls, marble floors and shelves, and in some a central fountain to keep things cool in summer. Shallow pans and tubs were used to pour the milk into, skimmers then removed the cream that settled on top, and this was either stored in vases or churned in tubs to make butter and cheese. Heated pipes would help keep the temperature steady in winter at 50-55 degrees while there would usually be a cleaning area or a separate scullery next door for washing the utensils, pans and dishes. In some houses the dairy work was carried out in the scullery with the dairy itself just being used for storage, a role it played increasingly as during the 19th century more products were bought in from outside rather than made on site.

▓ BREWHOUSE

Another important production room was the brewhouse, for in the days before safe drinking water, beer was drunk at mealtimes including breakfast. The building or room was tall in order to accommodate the coppers, and was usually distinguished by louvre openings high up for ventilation. It would be positioned to provide as easy access as possible for the deliveries of malt and hops, and to the trap door and chute which led to the beer cellar under the house.

FIG 9.15: *A diagram of the basic brewing process. (1) Water is heated to just below boiling point in a large copper with a fire beneath the tank and a doorway below this from which to remove the ashes. (2) The water is poured into the mash tun and malt added to produce wort which is poured into the underback below. This mashing process would usually be performed a second and third time, producing progressively weaker brews. (3) The wort is pumped up into either the original copper or as in this example into a second one and is boiled up with hops. (4) The final mixture is run off into cooling trays and then into casks for storage.*

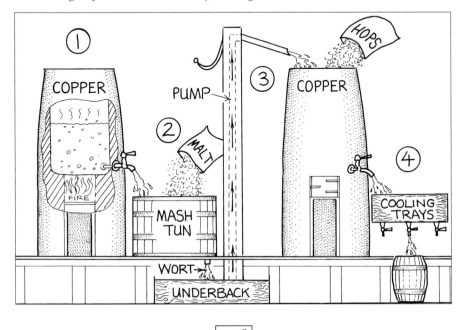

The beer produced was varied in strength depending on its intended use. Small or table beer was made from the weaker wort produced in the final third mash and was consumed as we would drink water and pop today, by everyone in the house. A medium strength brew called ale was made from the second mash while a strong ale or malt liquor was produced by adding extra malt into the first mash. This latter brew was usually for special occasions like the birth of an heir, when the ale was bottled and then stored until his coming of age celebrations when it was drunk! Brewing was best done in the colder months of the year from October to March, which was a problem as the weakest beer might only last a few weeks.

❈ SCULLERY

The word comes from the French *escuele*, meaning dish, which in turn was derived from the Latin word *scutella*, a salver, and hence is the room used for washing up plates and dishes. In the country house it was more versatile and a lot of the messy tasks like peeling, chopping and washing vegetables, preparing meat for roasting and gutting fish were done here. It is usually found next door to the kitchen.

In the typical 19th century scullery there would be sinks, preferably under the window so that those washing up had the best light in which to make sure there was no dirt left on the crockery, cutlery or utensils. In country houses you can find some shallow stone sinks, or wooden ones with exposed planks of teak or lined with lead, but usually by this date earthenware or china sinks were used with wooden draining boards to the sides and plate racks above. In the days before centrally heated water was available, a separate boiler or one built into a range was essential, while the

latter could also be used for some cooking tasks. There would have also been a pump for cold water until a tank in a tower in the house or nearby enabled it to be supplied under the pressure of gravity to taps emerging out of the wall above the sink.

❈ BUTTERY AND PANTRY

It was usual in medieval houses to have a buttery and pantry side by side at the opposite end of the hall from the dais and solar (see fig 8.1). The word buttery, which is derived from the same source as 'butt' or 'bottle', was where the casks of beer and other drinks were stored while they were being dispensed; long term storage would usually be in the cellar or outbuilding. The word pantry is derived from the Latin for bread, *panis*, and was originally where the grain and bread were kept. Both rooms were close to the hall so that these staple parts of the meal could be easily distributed.

The pantry was the responsibility of the pantler while the buttery was the responsibility of the butler! Although the latter's name survived the buttery itself faded from use, its role being taken over by the butler's pantry. This is not to be confused with the pantry which still appears in later houses, being used for the storage of dairy products and some cooked dishes as well as bread, although in Victorian houses it was often called the dry larder.

❈ LARDERS

The larder (from the Latin *lardum* meaning bacon) was originally an outbuilding where the raw meat was salted and stored. In the later country houses it could exist alongside the pantry, though increasingly by the 19th century there would be a number of larders for specific uses. The wet larder

FIG 9.16: BRODSWORTH HALL, SOUTH YORKSHIRE: *An old wooden octagonal game larder set in the shade of trees just behind the service block.*

was the one where pieces of meat were prepared and stored (it was called a 'butchery' if whole carcases were brought in), the dry larder had a similar role to the pantry, while fish and bacon larders are self explanatory. Game larders were often a separate round or octagonal structure where deer and birds were hung up, but by the late 19th century when shoots could bag thousands of game birds at a time, larger rooms were required, some with a primitive form of refrigeration.

The larder had to be cool and is often found on the north of the building, or if not it usually has overhanging eaves or plants shading its walls, while wet cloth might be thrown over the roof in the hottest of weather. Windows could be part or fully covered in gauze to permit a through draught but keep out insects. Around the whitewashed or tiled walls there would be slate, brick or marble shelves with hooks in the roof for hanging meat and perhaps an ice box for fish and cool dishes.

✳ CELLARS

The cellar was principally where wine and beer was stored, and due to their high value and the cool temperatures they required the best place for them was below the main house. They were convenient here for the owner of the house, and for the butler who could keep a close eye on the contents of the cellar and then store the drinks ready for serving in his pantry which was usually close by.

Cellars usually have a low vaulted ceiling (made up of brick or stone arches) and pillars, which helped take the load from the rooms above.

There may have been separate cellars for beer, with the barrels (originally with willow hoops, but later with iron ones) containing the servants' weak beer and the owner's stronger ale. The huge quantities of coal which 18th and 19th

century houses consumed means that there may have been a large store for this in the basement as well. Trap doors are to be found on the outside giving access to the cellar for deliveries, including those from the brewhouse.

▩ SERVANTS' HALL

As the owner distanced himself from his household and they in turn became wage earning servants of a general, lower status, separate servants' halls were provided. This meant that the staff could eat their meals among the service rooms, out of sight of the lord and his guests and not cluttering up his splendid new marble and stone entrance hall! Sometimes called the common hall, these rooms were furnished with a long table and in some a little beer barrel on wheels which could run up and down it for the dispensing of drinks. The walls might have portraits as at Erddig, near Wrexham, where the Yorke family commissioned paintings of ten of their staff.

▩ UPPER SERVANT ROOMS

Although the senior servants would dine with the other staff, they would then retire to one of their private rooms. The butler's pantry was usually in the main house, close to the dining room so he could take charge of the serving of food, but also with convenient access to the cellars and the main entrance. Within it could be found the containers of drink, table linen, crockery, cutlery and glasses which were in use, and perhaps a brick safe in which the more precious pieces would be stored. There would also be space, materials and often two sinks for cleaning these items and polishing the silver. As it served additionally as his office and living room, a table, chairs, wash-basin, fireplace and a bed could be

FIG 9.17: *A feature of fish larders, before the days of refrigerators, was an ice box which was used for storing fish and cold dishes. Ice from the estate ice house was put into the compartment at the side which cooled the lead-lined interior.*

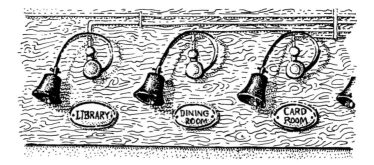

FIG 9.18: *A line of bells would have hung near to the butler's pantry to tell him in which room service was required.*

found crammed into what was often only a twelve by twelve foot room!

It was only really in the later 17th century that women started to take a significant role within the country house and the housekeeper first appears. Her accommodation was usually positioned near or between the service rooms where she could keep an eye on the staff, and with a door leading directly into the stillroom. The bulk of the crockery could be stored here, shelves later with glass fronts lined the walls or a separate china store would be close by, and she was also responsible for repairing and storing the table linen that was not in use at the time. Again as it was an office and sitting room there would be similar contents to those in the butler's pantry. Most houses would have had a steward who was responsible for the running of the estate, and he would usually have been provided with his own room, while the cook would generally use the housekeeper's room for office work.

▩ LAUNDRY

The early laundry or washroom usually had a large copper for boiling clothes and a pump to bring in water, while the washing in some cases was simply draped over hedges and lawns outside to dry. Later houses would often have two rooms. Firstly, a wet laundry where the washing took place, still with boilers providing hot water and a vent in the roof to let the steam out. The dry laundry was where the airing, ironing and folding was done and it would contain drying racks suspended from the ceiling, a range or stove on which the irons could be heated and a large table which would have been covered with sheeting when in use. The centre of the room was often dominated by a box mangle, a large flat-bed trough which when filled with stones pressed down onto a bed below and flattened partially dry linen in between (it was not used to wring out water from freshly washed fabric).

FIG 9.19: COGGES MANOR FARM MUSEUM, OXFORDSHIRE: *A shallow stone sink and pump with various pieces of equipment used in washing which could be found in the laundry or washroom.*

▩

As you can see from the plan in fig 9.1, these service rooms were organised like a production line to take the raw ingredients produced on the estate in at one end and supply a wide variety of meals at the other. By the late 19th century though, food and domestic supplies were increasingly coming from a local wholesaler and hence there was less need for areas to process raw ingredients. After the First World War most country house owners found the huge kitchens and suites of service rooms far too large for their greatly reduced household, and thus converted a smaller room into a new compact kitchen. More recently the original service rooms have been used to house tea rooms and restaurants, but now with a growing interest in how the mechanics of a stately home operated behind the scenes they are being refitted and opened for view, allowing visitors to see the tasks the household staff had to perform and the conditions in which they worked.

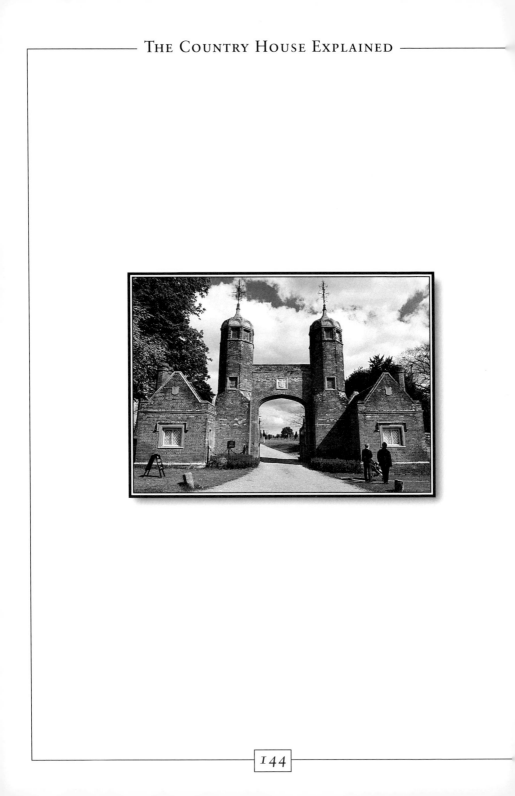

SECTION
III

THE GARDEN
AND
ESTATE

CHAPTER 10

Gardens and Parks

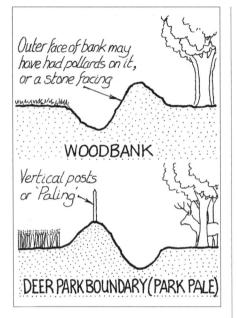

Outer face of bank may have had pollards on it, or a stone facing

WOODBANK

Vertical posts or 'Paling'

DEER PARK BOUNDARY (PARK PALE)

FIG 10.1: *Deer park boundaries or park pales (from the paling or fencing which ran along the top of the bank) can still be found today within country house estates. Earthworks like these can be difficult to identify but a deer park would have the bank on the outer side of an inner ditch to stop the animals jumping out, whereas a woodbank (another common boundary dug around a medieval wood) had the bank on the inside to keep livestock out.*

▨ MEDIEVAL GARDENS

As with the country house itself the land surrounding it changed over the centuries from being purely utilitarian to becoming an attractive display of the owner's prestige and taste. Early gardens attached to medieval monasteries were small enclaves with herbs and flowers grown for medicinal purposes and were usually close to the infirmary. Castles and fortified manor houses may have had areas of rough grass on which games could be played, with arbours, raised flowerbeds and trees surrounded by wattle or wooden fencing. As defence was still a primary concern when building these structures the perimeter wall or moat would have limited the extent of the garden. Despite this, recent evidence has shown that some medieval gardens extended beyond the confines of fortifications, with arrangements of water features, banks and driveways (not dissimilar to 18th century landscape gardens) appearing around some important palatial houses.

Of greater importance to the lord of the manor at this stage, though, was hunting and most aspired to laying out their own deer parks near their house. These reached a peak in the 13th century when there were some 3,000 parks across the country, each enclosing up to 200 acres. They would often be established within an existing wood on the lord's own land and tend to be a roughly circular tract of land enclosed within a ditch and bank with a hedge or fence along the top.

FIG 10.2: ASHDOWN PARK, OXFORDSHIRE: *This low bank running from the foreground, through the fences left of centre, and then up the hill between the fields, is the remains of a deer park boundary (park pale). The interior of the park is to the right and there are the faint signs of the ditch which would have kept the animals within it on that side of the bank.*

⬚TUDOR, ELIZABETHAN AND STUART GARDENS

During the 16th and early 17th century the changing role of the country house from an inward-looking, defensive building to an outgoing display of wealth was reflected in the gardens which grew around them. They became a place of leisure, with games, plays and masques acted out upon their lawns, and contemplative walks taken between flowerbeds and through arbours. Renaissance features like symmetry appear in the garden with blocks of low box hedging extending out along a straight axis in line with the centre of the façade of the house. These knot gardens contained geometric patterns while other features around the garden could have been cut or shaped to reflect the Elizabethans' love of secret symbols.

The old medieval moats and fishponds which had previously served a practical use were now incorporated into the design for ornamental purposes. The garden was further decorated with sundials, brightly painted statues and ornamental rails. Mazes grew in popularity, although at this date they were laid out in low hedges which the viewer could see over. The tall-hedged maze, correctly termed a labyrinth, was a later development.

Raised walkways and mounts, usually on the outer edge, were an essential feature from which the garden below and the surrounding countryside could be admired. New stone and brick walls replaced the old perimeter wooden fences, beyond which the trees which were banished from the garden could be found. As stag hunting declined

FIG 10.3: LITTLE MORETON HALL, CHESHIRE: *A recreated knot garden based on an Elizabethan design with the lighter gravel filling the pattern while the grass in the foreground was walked upon. Note how in this 16th century example the garden is not lined up with the centre of what is still an asymmetrical house. In the next century the new parterre designs would line up with the middle of the symmetrical Restoration houses.*

somewhat in popularity, many of the old deer parks were returned to agriculture, although some were retained and even a few new ones were created. Others were finally abandoned after boundaries were damaged and deer lost during the Civil

War, and by the end of the later 17th century there were new fashions for fox hunting and shooting.

✳ RESTORATION GARDENS

The Royalists returning from the Continent upon the Restoration of the Monarchy in 1660 brought with them new ideas in garden design. At first they tried to recreate the huge layouts they had seen in France, albeit on a smaller scale. Flat, rectangular beds of low hedging with flowers and coloured gravels called parterres (a French word meaning 'on the ground') spread out from the house on a much larger scale than the previous knot gardens. Terraces

with balustrades, rectangular water features, and topiary cut into geometric shapes were among the features to be found. Within the restrictions of the landscape the garden was made as flat as possible, so the old mounds and raised walkways were no longer used.

With the accession to the throne of William and Mary in 1688, Dutch gardens from the new King's homeland became fashionable. These were usually smaller than their French counterparts, with more elaborate detailing, trees in tubs, and lead statues while long rectangular stretches of water or canals with cascades and fountains were still popular. There was even a mania for

FIG 10.4: LITTLE MORETON HALL: *The photograph on the left shows the remains of a 16th century mount with the boundary hedge behind running along the edge of the old moat. The drawing on the right shows how it may have originally looked with some form of shelter or summerhouse on top accessed by a spiral path lined with low hedges. From here the owner and his guests could admire the gardens or look over the wooden fencing to the countryside beyond.*

tulips. Many shrubs were grown purely for their foliage and were known as 'greens'. In winter they were brought indoors to the 'greenhouse' which at this date was not the glasshouse we are familiar with but a conventional building, often with accommodation above for the gardener. The value of light to plant growth was not appreciated by horticulturalists at this date.

Now the garden could also expand over the dormant medieval boundaries and, in a show of control over nature, straight avenues of trees burst out of the confines of the garden into the surrounding countryside and old deer parks. Formal arrangements of high, clipped hedges in geometric patterns called a 'wilderness' were laid out for walking within, although where this name survives today the area tends to be more appropriately natural and wooded.

▓ GEORGIAN GARDENS

Although formal gardens continued to be laid out throughout this period, the 18th century is better known for the landscape gardens which engulfed huge tracts of land. The inspiration for these new informal gardens had come from the pictures of 17th century artists like Claude. These paintings showed mystical, ancient lands with expanses of lawn rolling down to lakes surrounded by ruined castles, towers and temples with distant mountains shrouded in a golden glow. The garden designers who transferred these images into the English

---

FIG 10.5: POWIS CASTLE, POWYS: *A view from the terraces with their balustrades and statues over this late 17th century garden. The plain lawn to the right originally contained parterres, geometric-shaped ponds with fountains, statues and a cascade flowing down from the now densely wooded 'wilderness' beyond.*

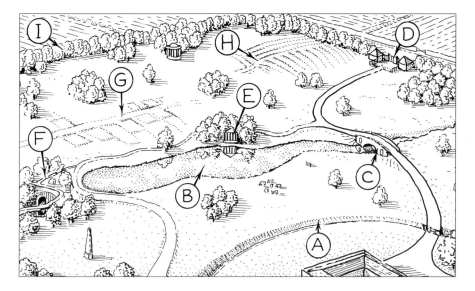

FIG 10.6: *An overview showing features you might find today in an 18th century landscape garden. The house is near the bottom right corner and is surrounded by a ha-ha (A). In the middle distance is a serpentine lake (B) formed by damming the local stream, which is crossed by a Classical styled bridge (C) carrying the main drive from the similarly treated gate lodges (D). From the drive visitors can view the various eye-catching buildings, including a mock temple (E) overlooking the lake, or wander down to the grotto (F) formed around the waterfall created on the dam. In order to create this great park the lord of the manor had to remove the old village, which was finally done when he had an Enclosure Act passed through Parliament, reorganising the old open fields into new rectangular blocks and moving the farmers within the village to new isolated farmhouses out in their fields. Traces of the old village (G) and the ridge and furrows of the open fields (H) can still be seen while the new boundary hedge (I) follows the straight lines of the new fields beyond.*

countryside were increasingly professional men, the most famous of which was Lancelot 'Capability' Brown, who gained his name from his habit of informing clients that their gardens had 'capabilities'.

In order to create these vast expanses of private parkland the owner would have to remove villages and turn over fields. The dispossessed locals were sometimes fortunate enough to be rehoused in a new village well out of view of the house, but many were simply evicted and moved to the towns to find work in the new factories and mills. The land they left behind was transformed into a gently rolling parkland interspersed with clumps of trees and large serpentine lakes (in a long, curving shape like a serpent) and bounded by a thick band of trees. Despite these subsequent changes, the faint banks and

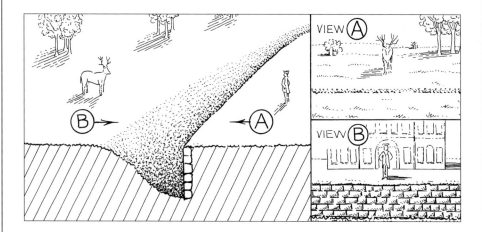

FIG 10.7: *A cut through view of a ha-ha formed by a brick or stone retaining wall and a grass slope running into its base. This clever device meant that the deer looking towards the house would see view (B) with a wall preventing its advance, while the owner looking out would see view (A) where the ha-ha is virtually invisible, giving unbroken views over the park.*

ditches which marked their homes and fields can still be seen in many parks today.

The 17th century formal garden was designed to be viewed on foot from fixed points with straight avenues leading the eye into the distance. The landscape garden, though, was to be appreciated by guests arriving in a carriage, so clumps of trees and eye-catching towers and temples were arranged so that the view changed slowly to reveal distant objects as visitors were driven along the winding road. You can still get a similar effect today in a car, where these gardens have survived.

Another aspect of landscape gardens was that the park came right up to the front door of the house, ideally with any formal flowerbeds removed. The problem with this was that the deer and livestock in the park could wander right up to the house, so the solution was to build a ha ha, a ditch with a vertical wall, around the house so that it stopped the animals getting too close without spoiling the view.

▨ REGENCY GARDENS

By the turn of the 19th century the aristocracy were becoming bored with the plain expanses of green and brown and a new breed of designers like Humphrey Repton had to spice things up again. Formal beds of flowers, gravel walkways and terraces reappeared around the house while thicker blocks of trees with greater variety were laid out in the park. These schemes were often smaller than the preceding landscapes of Brown, so in order that the owner would appear to have a larger park, the outer boundary of trees was broken and eye-catching features were erected on distant higher ground to be viewed through these openings.

FIG 10.8: BRODSWORTH HALL, SOUTH YORKSHIRE: *Quarry gardens were popular picturesque features in the late 18th and early 19th century. This example was dug out to provide stone for the original house, although it is being restored with a planting scheme which dates from when the new house was erected in the 1860s.*

This was a time of growing appreciation of Nature and the Picturesque, so ruined garden features, grottos, and furniture and buildings made from bark-covered wood were popular.

▨ VICTORIAN GARDENS

As with the profusion of styles that reigned in house design through this period, the Victorian garden could take any number of forms, usually from historic or exotic sources. Italianate styles, for instance, were popular in the mid 1800s featuring a return to balustraded terraces, statues, fountains, and rigid layouts of flowerbeds although these were now filled with richly coloured flowers rather than the limited palette available to the original Renaissance gardener. Many gardens were compartmentalised, with different areas given over to formal planting, water features, scenes from distant lands, or woodland.

Among the features that distinguish a Victorian garden is the importance given to the contents rather than structure of the layout. Trees and shrubs from all around the world were now being transported here and could be propagated in the new temperature-controlled glasshouses. They were laid out in a way that would display the

FIG 10.9: BRODSWORTH HALL: *A distinctive Victorian garden with beds full of rich-coloured flowers, cedars and nearest of all a monkey puzzle tree, one of the popular conifers grown in this period. The mixed species of trees which stand to the left of the house shrouded it from the outside. Rather than travelling through open parkland as was common in the 18th century, Victorian guests would approach through this barrier of woodland, along a drive lined with clipped evergreens, before suddenly emerging in front of the house.*

FIG 10.10: WADDESDON MANOR, BUCKINGHAMSHIRE: *This late Victorian, French chateau house had a matching 17th century styled garden which is similar to the parterre that would have stood on the plain lawn at Powis Castle in fig 10.5.*

individual plant at its best rather than for a collective effect. Most significant were trees, especially conifers, which along with rhododendrons formed distinctive dark, dank, cathedral-like winding avenues. Some were collected to form arboretums, or if only conifers were grown they were known as pinetums. Rock and wild gardens, shrubberies and ferneries were also popular towards the end of the century. The increasingly large teams of gardeners were aided by new technology like lawnmowers, glasshouses and new drainage methods.

Today most gardens around country houses have been reshaped numerous

FIG 10.11: *The walled or kitchen garden was an essential part of any self-supporting country estate. Its tall boundary wall sheltered the interior, so fruit trees could grow up its walls, with herbs and vegetables in the beds and borders.*

times and hence would all have a Victorian feel to them if it was not for the efforts during the 20th century to restore many to something like an original form. No genuinely complete garden from the 16th or 17th century survives in England but, thanks to these restoration projects, there are many very good examples of period gardens to visit.

Garden Buildings

▨ ORANGERIES

It was not until the 19th century that the need for light was fully appreciated by horticulturalists, but those who in the late 17th century followed the fashion of growing orange trees in pots knew they needed protection from the cold. They started to construct garden buildings suitably called 'orangeries', in which the trees could be kept in winter but which also could be used for social functions in summer when the pots were placed outside. These early types were often built into a terrace with just a row of windows exposed at the front. In the 18th century orangeries were usually rectangular or large semi-circles up against a wall, made of brick with stone cladding and covered by a solid roof. There would be a row of south facing,

usually sash windows set within a row of archways (a loggia), so that the lower half of the sash could be raised high enough for someone to enter, thus there was little need for a large door.

While the trees were outside during the growing season the fact that the roof and rear of the building allowed no light through was not a problem. By the later 18th century, though, imported exotic plants which required cover all year round were becoming popular and growth would therefore lean towards the light at the front. This led to glass roofs being constructed over existing and newly built orangeries to solve the problem.

FIG 10.12: TATTON PARK, CHESHIRE: *The Conservatory at Tatton Park was designed in 1818 but unlike later versions it was a freestanding stone and glass structure and still holds exotic greenery today.*

CONSERVATORIES, GREENHOUSES AND WINTER GARDENS

Although the conservatory and greenhouse had existed previously and originally referred to the same type of building, it was in the Victorian age that they became an essential feature of any country house garden. The familiar white-painted metal-framed glasshouses which they built could receive the light essential for the new imported exotic plants. Transporting these was made easier after 1833 with the invention of the Wardian Case. This was a mini glasshouse with a carrying handle, in which the young plants could be brought home. They would then have been transferred into an outer greenhouse before being planted later in the main glass structure.

The decorative conservatory was usually attached to the house while the

FIG 10.13: WITLEY COURT, WORCESTERSHIRE: *Although it was fixed to the main house and accessible via a door just to the right of the left-hand pair of columns this Victorian conservatory was also known as the orangery (this was perhaps because the row of columns and arches, a loggia, looked similar to a typical orangery). Built in the 1850s it originally had a massive glass roof and window panes inserted directly into the columns (you can just make out the white line running vertically up the inner of the two columns where the glass was fitted). It contained a wide range of tropical plants set in beds between marble floors, although much of this was lost when the house was gutted by fire in 1937.*

greenhouse was a more humble, painted timber or metal-framed building usually out in the walled garden. Gardeners believed that the sun should hit the glass at 90° and two schools of thought developed – either recommending that the roof should be curved or domed, or that it should be formed into rows of ridges and furrows. Both of these had been made possible with the availability of cast iron and large sheets of glass, although timber became popular for some of the structure in the late 19th century. Hot water heating systems were used, while heat might also be obtained from a fireplace and flue on the other side of the rear wall. The high maintenance these buildings required meant that many were abandoned or burnt down after the First World War and it is the earlier orangeries or reconstructed conservatories that are generally seen today.

▓ FOLLIES, MONUMENTS AND GROTTOS

There have always been garden structures within which to socialise, contemplate or appreciate the surrounding flora. In the 16th and 17th centuries there were banqueting houses where diners could retire after a meal and enjoy sweets, and gazebos or summerhouses from which they could admire the owner's clever garden designs and discuss their hidden meanings. It was in the 18th century, though, that the strange, monumental and exotic structures that form an important part of many country house tours today were erected.

Follies – the term that we generally apply to these expensive garden structures – were not always as useless as the name implies, although to the local in his timber framed hovel they must have

FIG 10.14: CHISWICK HOUSE, LONDON: *This rotunda was just one of the buildings featured in this early 18th century garden, elements of which were used in the later, fully developed landscape parks.*

FIG 10.15: SHUGBOROUGH, STAFFORDSHIRE: *This Chinese House was one of the earliest in the country, built in 1747 and designed from sketches made in the Orient by Sir Piercy Brett, the Second in Command to Admiral Lord Anson, whose elder brother owned Shugborough.*

seemed an extravagant waste of time. To the owner they were an important part of the landscape park design, acting as eye-catching features for the travelling guests and venues for garden parties, music recitals and social meetings.

Although the main house had to be built with strict rules and fashions in mind, architects were given a much freer range with garden structures. Some were copies of the round towers that featured in the paintings of artists like Claude, which had inspired the landscape garden in the first place. Others were Roman and later Greek temples, triumphal arches and rotundas, pieces of the Ancient World recreated for the owner fresh back from his Grand Tour. Gothic architecture reappears on the country estate in the mid 1700s.

In the later 18th century the Picturesque movement and the growing appreciation of all things British increased the number of sham castles, ruined structures and fake prehistoric stone circles erected. Another source for inspiration was the exotic Far East, with Chinese pagodas and bridges proving especially popular. Statues and monuments also featured in these park schemes and it is not unusual to find an impressive stone pinnacle erected to the memory of a favourite pet! Grottos with shell-lined caves, set in small valleys which were often formed as part of the scheme to dam a stream in order to create the lake, feature throughout the 18th century.

These structures did not have to be confined to the park itself. Towers and

FIG 10.16: STOWE LANDSCAPE GARDENS, BUCKINGHAMSHIRE: *Stowe's Landscape Gardens are home to the largest collection of follies in England and possibly the world! This triangular Gothic Temple of 1742 was one of the first to use this style, although Stowe House – as with most others at the time – was strictly Classical. It shows how the architects, in this case Gibbs, could cast off their Palladian chains and have a bit of fun in the garden. The use of this 'barbarian' style still had to be justified though, so it was dedicated to the 'Liberty of our Ancestors' with its triangular plan said to represent the Whig principles of Enlightenment, Liberty and Constitution. It is not known whether the owner, Lord Cobham, knew about the Triangular Lodge at nearby Rushton, which represented Thomas Tresham's Catholic faith, a dangerous association only a few years before Bonnie Prince Charlie's Jacobite uprising.*

FIG 10.17: MOW COP, CHESHIRE: *One of the first sham castle towers, built in 1754 as an eye-catcher to be viewed from nearby Rode Hall. It was intended as a summerhouse and originally had an inverted cone roof, so that it could be used as a beacon, it is said.*

ruins were built on distant hills, thus giving the owner from his gardens in the valley below the impression that he owned and had influence over a huge tract of land. These buildings of great expense can more justifiably be called follies as they were fanciful whims which, being inconveniently placed, must have had limited use. Some of the monuments and follies found today isolated in fields may not have been built under the above circumstances, however, but may be the only part of these once great parks left behind when the estate shrank in the 20th century and the land was returned to agriculture.

In the 19th century more enclosed and compartmentalised garden, distant eye-catching features were less important although small buildings from a historic period or distant land added the signature to a garden theme, with Chinese, Egyptian and Swiss structures proving popular.

FIG 10.18: SHUGBOROUGH, STAFFORDSHIRE: *The Doric Temple dates from the 1760s and is believed to have been designed by James 'Athenian' Stuart. On his return from studying the Ancient remains in Greece he produced 'The Antiquities of Athens' which featured the first accurate drawings of Greek architecture and not the Roman versions that everyone had been using up to that date. It was only after this that the plain Doric columns, which run directly into the base on this truncated temple, appeared in England.*

FIG 10.19: BRIDGEWATER MONUMENT, ASHRIDGE, HERTFORDSHIRE: *A huge Doric column of 1832, raised in memory to the 3rd Duke of Bridgewater, who was credited with sparking the mania in the late 18th century for building canals.*

FIG 10.20: BIDDULPH GRANGE GARDEN, STAFFORDSHIRE: *An exceptional restored Victorian garden where you are transported via tunnels and screens to the far ends of the earth. There are sphinxes flanking the Egyptian doorway (left), an ornate timber building known as the Cheshire Cottage (middle), and a taste of China with a brightly painted bridge (right). There are also scenes from Italy, a Scottish glen, and an arboretum and pinetum, the entrance to the latter being via the Cheshire Cottage (note the pine cone to the right of it in the middle photograph).*

FIG 10.21: CHISWICK HOUSE, LONDON: *A classically styled bridge with a flat, segmented arch, a balustraded parapet and arched niches either side. This is very typical of the type of bridge which features in numerous 18th century landscape gardens.*

⊞ BRIDGES

Eighteenth century landowners who flooded the valley in front of their house to create a large serpentine lake would now require a bridge by which to cross it. Although they copied Roman architecture almost to the letter for the houses and follies, the crude forms of their bridges seems not to have appealed and technology had by this time developed segmented arched structures that could span a greater length. These more graceful bridges would often carry the main drive to the house and typically featured balustrades and arched niches. Pedestrians might find something more ornamental like the famous Palladian bridge which was copied at a number of houses.

FIG 10.22: STOWE LANDSCAPE GARDENS: *A Palladian styled bridge which again features in 18th century landscape gardens.*

CHAPTER 11

The Estate

Estate Buildings and Features

▦ STABLES AND COACH-HOUSES

Every country house would have had stables in which were housed saddle horses, coach horses, cart horses and foals. Most seem to date from the 17th to the 19th century and they are usually built around a courtyard in which other estate trades like a blacksmith's or joiner's workshop may also be found. The exterior was symmetrical with brick being popular in the 17th century and stone or stuccoed coverings in the 18th century, while in the middle was a large archway, high enough for coaches to pass under. There would be a tack room which always had a fireplace to protect the leather and ironwork from damp, while above the stalls there would be a hay loft. A distinctive feature of nearly all stables was the cupola above the main high-arched entrance with a clock and bell striking every hour.

Coaches had become popular with all levels of the gentry by the late 17th century, and most would have two, a basic one for everyday use and another of greater luxury. Earlier coaches had only leather flaps or curtains to protect

FIG 11.1: DUNHAM MASSEY, CHESHIRE: *The North Stable Block (actually a coach-house) with its distinctive white cupola and the South Block just out of view to the right date from the 1720s and are still surrounded by the old moat which was dug sometime before 1400. The North Block originally housed a brewhouse and bakehouse with a large space for the carriage horses, while the riding horses, cart horses and dairy cows were kept in the South Block.*

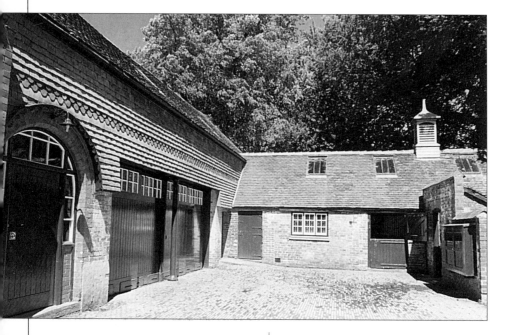

FIG 11.2: WIGHTWICK MANOR, WEST MIDLANDS: *Part of the stable complex.*

passengers from the elements but by this time these had been replaced with glass windows while suspension improved the ride. It was not until the 18th century development of turnpike roads that the journey became more comfortable and quicker. At first coaches were kept in the stables or even in a barn, but from the 17th century purpose-built structures with tall double doors were usually part of the stable complex.

❖ HUNTING, SHOOTING AND RACING

Hunting has remained the most popular pastime for nobles from long before the Normans placed vast areas of the country under Forest Law to protect deer for the sport. The quarry though has changed over the centuries with deer and hares which were still popular in the 16th and 17th century being superseded in the 18th century by the fox. This brought together all ranks of the estate. The Master, often the lord himself, led the pack, while the Huntsman was responsible for looking after the hounds and Hunt Servants organised the event. It was at this time that most of the trappings and traditions associated with the sport were introduced. Some of the estates and surrounding landscape had to be adapted to make it suitable for the fox. For instance, gorse was planted in Lincolnshire, artificial earths were dug in Essex and special fences flanked by hedges in Leicestershire. Kennels for the hounds had to be built, usually on one of the estate farms.

Developments in the gun meant that from the late 17th century shooting replaced hawking as the method of hunting game birds. By the 19th century it had become the chosen sport of the aristocracy with the pheasant replacing other fowl as the preferred quarry. The main growth in pheasant shooting was during the agricultural depressions of 1815-1840 and 1880-1900 when, for economic reasons as well as fashion, increased numbers of the bird were reared with the aid of coverts, strips of existing woodland held back from the plough or new purpose-made plantations (they were also used for foxes).

Another favoured pastime in the 18th century was horse racing with the addiction to gambling being the ruin of many a young lord. Steeplechasing, literally racing towards a steeple of a church (as no flags or guides could be used, it was the best landmark to follow), started in 1752. Racing horses around a flat track though was known to have taken place during the Roman occupation. Its rise in popularity through the 18th century led to the creation of numerous courses, even on modern day protected sites like Runnymede in Surrey and Port Meadow in Oxford. Some estates also had a circular or oval track and records of these can be found on old estate maps.

▨ HOME FARM

In the medieval estate there was a central area of land which was called the demesne; the produce grown on it was for the lord of the manor's table, while the remainder of the land provided a subsistence for the villagers. The farm buildings of the demesne would form

part of the complex around the manor house. Social changes in the 14th and 15th century meant that the villagers became rent-paying tenant farmers, while the nobles became landlords. As the land was reorganised by enclosure acts up until the 19th century, most of which were initiated by and benefited the larger tenant farmers and their landlords, new farms were established including a

FIG 11.3: NOSTELL PRIORY, WEST YORKSHIRE: *The stable block cupola which dates from the 1770s with a clock, bell and weather vane.*

Home Farm to manage the estate's own land. These were no longer built alongside the house, but at a suitable distance to keep farmyard smells away from aristocratic noses!

The fashion for nobles to become involved in agricultural improvement during the late 18th century produced a spate of new farm building featuring the latest technologies. The Home Farm of the estate had by the early and mid 19th century become more like an efficient factory production line rather than a rustic collection of barns. They would usually be formed around a courtyard, with brick or stone buildings containing some of the earliest farm machines. These were at first powered by a horse wheel (look for a round or polygonal structure on the side of the farm within which the animal walked round), a water or wind mill, and later by a steam engine, the chimney of which often survives today.

Other buildings on these model farms could have contained cattle stalls, stables, storerooms, poultry houses, cart sheds, and sometimes a dairy. The brewhouse and bakehouse might be here rather than in the service rooms, often next to each other. Outside there would be a house for the bailiff, steward or manager from which he could keep an eye on the farmhands' comings and goings.

DOVECOTES

The dovecote was another essential feature of the estate as it added to the variety of food available for the owner of the house, especially in winter. It was a round or square structure with a pointed roof and openings in the gables from which the birds could fly out. Inside, pigeons (doves were not, in fact, kept for this purpose as they lack homing tendencies) nested in recesses with some type of ladder arrangement for servants to gain access to them. Although some early examples of dovecotes do survive, most of those that you will find today date from the 17th to the 19th century.

FISHPONDS AND WARRENS

A set of ponds in which fish were reared for the lord's table was an essential feature of any medieval house. Although most were eventually abandoned or filled in, some were incorporated within later garden schemes. So if you find a number of long pools with one end wider than the other and arranged in tiers they may have originated as fishponds.

The medieval estate would also provide the house with another delicacy,

FIG 11.4: DUNHAM MASSEY, CHESHIRE: *An early 19th century dovecote in the centre of the farm courtyard.*

FIG 11.5: STANTON HARCOURT MANOR, OXFORDSHIRE: *The interior of a dovecote showing the tiny nesting holes between the brickwork for the pigeons. There would have been some type of ladder to enable the servants to gain access to the birds.*

rabbit, which was introduced by the Normans and bred in purpose-made low banks called warrens.

▦ CHURCH

Many country houses have a church standing nearby, this close proximity indicating that the site has been occupied by a substantial house in some cases even

FIG 11.6: STOWE LANDSCAPE GARDENS, BUCKINGHAMSHIRE: *This medieval parish church is all that is left from the old village of Stowe, which had finally been removed by 1719 to make way for Viscount Cobham's new landscape gardens. It dates from the 13th century although the curved roof on the chancel was added in the 1790s. It was surrounded by evergreens on purpose so that it would not spoil the view from the owner's new house and gardens, which it was now hidden in the middle of.*

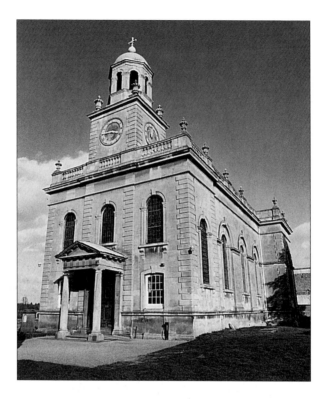

FIG 11.7: WITLEY COURT, WORCESTERSHIRE: *An 18th century Classical church with its distinctive rectangular form, semi-circular arched windows and clock tower with cupola. It had replaced an old, decaying medieval structure. The rather plain exterior is in stark contrast to the spectacular white and gold Rococo interior which is one of the finest in the country (see fig 7.8).*

before the Norman Conquest. Saxon nobles would often establish a church next to their halls as a status symbol in order to climb the social ladder. The village that is associated with the country house today may have been attracted to its site by the presence of the parish church and manor house.

In other situations the church may be all that is left from a village that was cleared out when the lord of the manor formed his landscape park. On the other hand the church itself could be a new building, especially in the Classical 18th century when a medieval Gothic pile would hardly sit correctly next to a Palladian mansion. Many of the extraordinary structures which date from this time though were only makeovers or were built upon the site of an older edifice. The Catholic Emancipation Act of 1829 also meant that suppressed

Catholic nobles could pray openly and fashionable Gothic brick churches appeared on some of their estates.

The owner of the house would often have a private chapel but would usually attend the parish church on a Sunday with his family, although they would expect a private set of pews and even a fireplace so that they did not have to suffer the sermon in discomfort! It was also the practice for the church and not the private room of prayer back in the house to hold the family monuments, usually in a side chapel or aisle. When the noble decided to move his seat to another of his houses, though, family burials would still take place in the church next to his original home.

▦ICE HOUSES

We take the cooling of food and drink for granted today, but before the arrival of refrigerators, it was a problem which only the wealthy could afford to solve. They could either buy ice from delivery men or collect their own and store it throughout the year. This latter solution

FIG 11.8: CAPESTHORNE HALL, CHESHIRE: *Under the shade of the trees is the entrance to the ice house (missing its doors). It stands near the end of a lake with a bank sloping down to a stream just out of view to the left, into which it could have drained.*

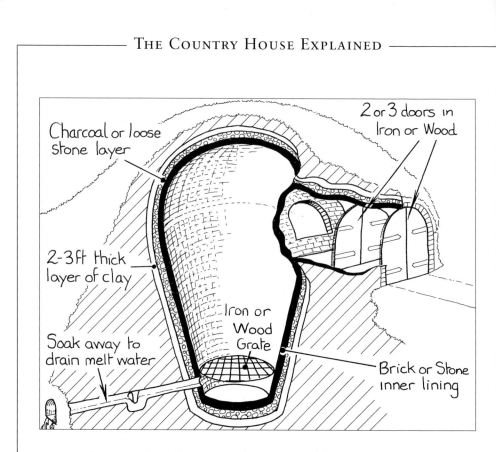

FIG 11.9: *A cut out of a 19th century ice house. A set of doors would lead to the access into the pit in which the ice was held. An iron or wood grate at the bottom allowed any melt water to drain off via the pipe while in this case a sandwich of brick, stone, charcoal and clay insulated the interior.*

was only possible if they had a large enough expanse of water, like a lake, and somewhere cool for storage, and hence – mainly in the 18th and 19th centuries – they erected ice houses.

The idea was that ice would be collected by estate workers from the frozen lake, pond or canal with hooks, mallets and rammers. It was then dragged along to the ice house where it would be broken up and compacted in the bottom of the pit with straw laid between for insulation. For the ice to last the whole year the position of the

house and its construction were critical. The pit was usually sited near the source of ice for convenience, usually built into a slope so that any melt water could flow out of the bottom, and was often surrounded by trees for shade. The insulated pit was covered by a brick dome with an air vent to reduce damp (which accelerated melting) with access through a small tunnel with at least two sets of doors to keep the interior cool.

The ice collected off the top of the lake would have been pretty mucky and

FIG 11.10: LAMBETH PALACE, LONDON: *Entry to the London residence of the Archbishop of Canterbury is via this large, five-storey gatehouse which is typical of larger medieval and Tudor structures.*

was therefore only used to cool bottles or was placed in ice boxes (see fig 9.17). It wasn't until imported ice was available from the mid 19th century that it was of good enough quality to be placed directly into drinks. Despite the arrival of refrigerators in the late 19th century, many ice houses continued to be used well into the 20th century.

GATEHOUSES AND LODGES

The most vulnerable point of castles, from which the country house descended, was the entrance, and hence large, towered structures with portcullises and drawbridges were erected. In the later medieval and Tudor houses it was still fashionable to surround your house with defensive

FIG 11.11: MELFORD HALL, SUFFOLK: *This gateway has octagonal towers topped by ogee-shaped caps, a Tudor feature, but the pair of lodges at either side are more typical of the 17th and 18th century.*

features like moats and walls and to build a tall gatehouse, usually in brick with corner towers and battlements along the top. A senior member of the household would reside in the room above the gate while a porter controlled entry to the courtyard beyond (as is still the case at many ancient universities and colleges today).

The last gatehouses were built in the early 17th century. Subsequently, with the boundary of the park moving further and further away from the house, a pair of lodges either side of the entry to the main drive became the norm. Classically styled lodges in the 18th century and quaint Gothic or Italianate cottages in the 19th century usually housed an elderly member of the staff who, on the sound of the horn or whistle from an approaching coach, would open the gates.

FIG 11.12: SHARDELOES, BUCKINGHAMSHIRE: *One of a pair of lodges dating from the late 18th century with Classical pilasters and columns over the doorway and large sash windows.*

FIG 11.13: BLENHEIM PALACE, OXFORDSHIRE: *It was not just the main entrance to country houses that had elaborate gateways. The Woodstock Gate pictured here was designed by Hawksmoor in 1723 and takes the form of a triumphal arch from Ancient Rome, a building type which also features in many 18th century landscape parks.*

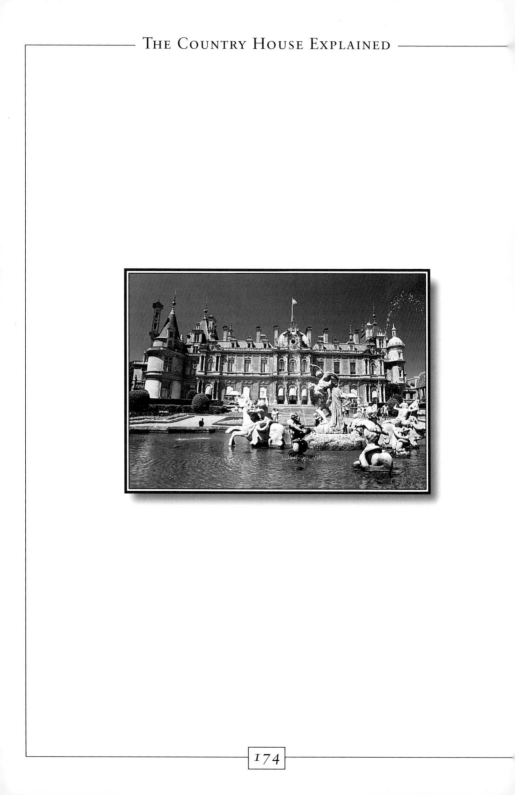

SECTION
IV

QUICK
REFERENCE
GUIDE

A time chart listing some of the principal architects and country houses (with the architect's initials in the house symbol if he is listed above). Please note that the dating, especially of early houses, is only approximate, and the boundaries between the styles would often overlap by a number of decades.

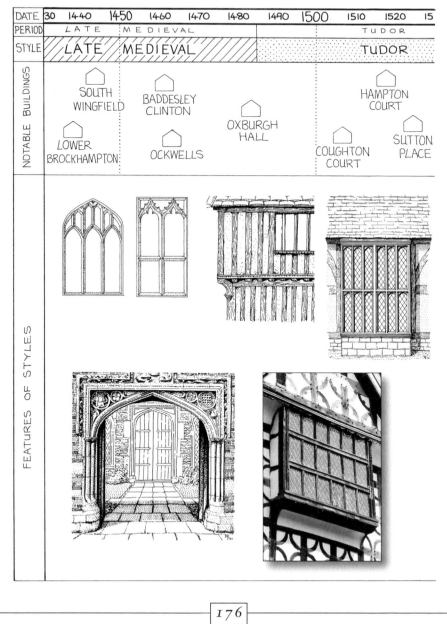

DATE	30	1440	1450	1460	1470	1480	1490	1500	1510	1520	15
PERIOD		LATE		MEDIEVAL				TUDOR			
STYLE		LATE	MEDIEVAL					TUDOR			

NOTABLE BUILDINGS

SOUTH WINGFIELD

BADDESLEY CLINTON

OXBURGH HALL

HAMPTON COURT

LOWER BROCKHAMPTON

OCKWELLS

COUGHTON COURT

SUTTON PLACE

FEATURES OF STYLES

NOTABLE COUNTRY HOUSE ARCHITECTS										

—John Smythson—

•——— Robert Smythson ———•

•—Inigo Jones—

•—Robert Lyminge—

| 30 | 1540 | 1550 | 1560 | 1570 | 1580 | 1590 | 1600 | 1610 | 1620 | 16 |

TUDOR	ELIZABETHAN	JACOBEAN

TUDOR | RENAISSANCE
(ELIZABETHAN PRODIGY HOUSE) | (JACOBEAN PRODIGY HOUSES)

BURGHLEY HOUSE

HARDWICK HALL R.S.

AUDLEY END

RAYNHAM HALL

LITTLE MORETON HALL

WOLLATON HALL R.S.

LONGLEAT R.S.

CONDOVER HALL

HATFIELD HOUSE R.L.

BLICKLING HALL R.L.

GEORGIAN CHAR

John Webb

Hugh May

Sir Roger Pratt

William Talman

Sir John Vanbrugh

Nicholas Hawksmoor

Lord Burlington

Colen Campbell

James Gibbs

30	1640	1650	1660	1670	1680	1690	1700	1710	1720	17
JACOBEAN	COMMONWEALTH		RESTORATION			WILLIAM + MARY	/ ANNE		GEORGIAN	

RENAISSANCE
(CAROLEAN)   (DUTCH STYLE)

BAROQUE

I.J.
WILTON HOUSE

R.P
COLESHILL
(Demolished)

H.M.
ELTHAM LODGE

SUDBURY HALL

BELTON HOUSE

W.T.
CHATSWORTH HOUSE

W.T.
UPPARK

J.V.
CASTLE HOWARD

N.H.
EASTON NESTON

J.V.
SEATON DELAVAL HALL

J.V.
BLENHEIM PALACE

L.B.
CHISWICK HOUSE

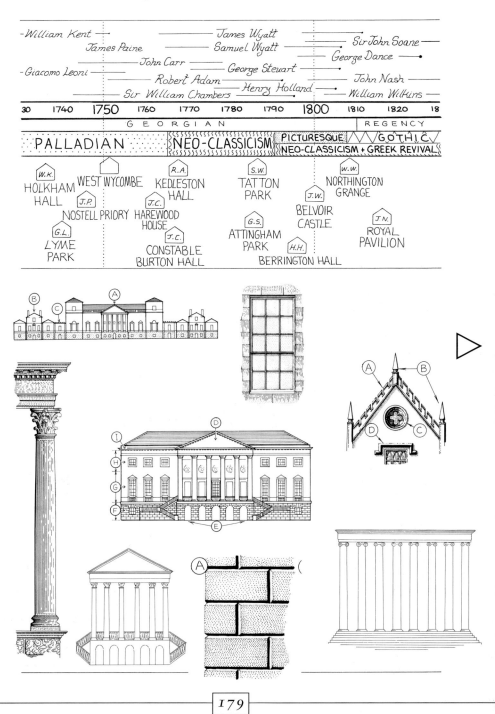

PALLADIAN · NEO-CLASSICISM · PICTURESQUE · GOTHIC
NEO-CLASSICISM + GREEK REVIVAL

-William Kent —
James Paine
-Giacomo Leoni
John Carr
Robert Adam
Sir William Chambers
James Wyatt
Samuel Wyatt
George Steuart
Henry Holland
Sir John Soane
George Dance
John Nash
William Wilkins

30   1740   1750   1760   1770   1780   1790   1800   1810   1820   18

G E O R G I A N   R E G E N C Y

W.K. HOLKHAM HALL   WEST WYCOMBE   R.A. KEDLESTON HALL   S.W. TATTON PARK   W.W. NORTHINGTON GRANGE
J.P. NOSTELL PRIORY   J.C. HAREWOOD HOUSE   J.W. BELVOIR CASTLE
G.L. LYME PARK   J.C. CONSTABLE BURTON HALL   G.S. ATTINGHAM PARK   J.N. ROYAL PAVILION
H.H. BERRINGTON HALL

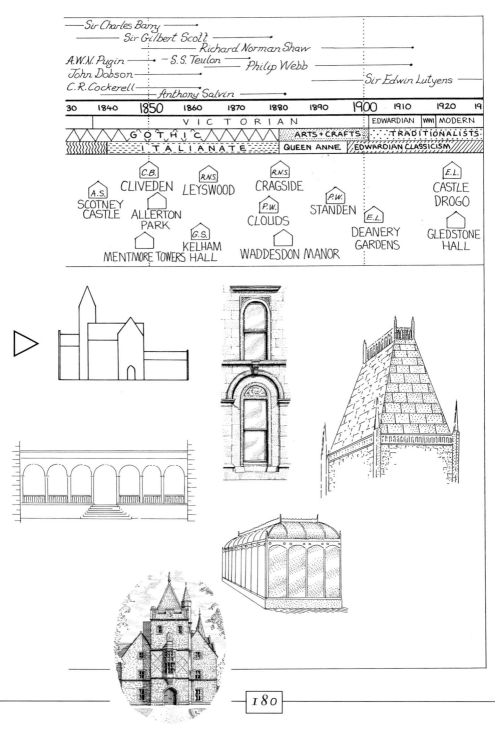

GLOSSARY

ABUTMENT: A wall which supports the arch of a bridge or a vaulted ceiling.

AISLE: A side space running along a hall and separated by a row of posts (hence aisled hall).

ANTHEMION: A decorative honeysuckle flower.

APSE: A semi-circular area at one end of a church or room (see fig 8.7C).

ARCADE: A row of arches and columns.

ARCHITRAVE: The lowest part of the entablature (see fig 4.13) and the surround of a doorway.

ASHLAR: A type of smooth stone masonry with fine joints.

ASTYLAR: A façade with no vertical features such as columns.

ATRIUM: A top lit court rising through a number of storeys.

BALUSTRADE: A row of decorated uprights (balusters) with a rail along the top.

BLIND: An arcade, balustrade or portico where the openings are filled in.

BOLECTION MOULDING: A curved shaped moulding used to cover the joint between two different surface levels. Popular in the late 17th and early 18th century and often found surrounding three sides of the opening of a fireplace.

BONDING: The way bricks are laid in a wall which can be recognised by the pattern made by the headers (short end of a brick) and stretchers (long side of a brick). Two common forms are English bond (see fig 5.17 right) with a row of stretchers above a row of headers, which was popular in the 16th and 17th century, and Flemish bond (see fig 5.17 left) with rows of alternate headers and stretchers, which largely replaced it by the 18th century.

CAPITAL: The decorated top of a column (see fig 4.13).

CARTOUCHE: A usually oval-shaped tablet featuring a coat of arms.

CARYATIDS: Female figures supporting an entablature (see fig 7.12).

CASEMENT: A window which is hinged at the side.

CASTELLATED: A battlemented feature (see fig 5.5A).

COADE STONE: A form of ceramic stone which was made in the late 18th and early 19th century and named after its original manufacturer Eleanor Coade. The recipe was subsequently lost.

COFFERED CEILING: A ceiling with sunken panels (coffers).

COLONNADE: A row of columns supporting an entablature.

CONSOLE: An ornamental bracket with an S-shaped centre.

CORNICE: The top section of an entablature (see fig 4.13) which also features around the top of interior and exterior walls.

CUPOLA: A small, domed, round or polygonal tower which stands on top of a roof or dome (see fig 3.19).

DAUB: A mixture of clay and mud (usually with straw or animal hair for increased strength) which was used to cover the wattle strips which filled in the gaps in a timber framed house.

DORMER WINDOW: An upright window set in the angle of the roof casting light into attic rooms which were usually used for sleeping quarters (from French verb 'to sleep').

DOUBLE PILE: A house which is two rooms deep.

DRIP MOULDING: A moulding running along the top of a window to protect it from rain.

EAVES: The roof overhang projecting over the wall.

ENFILADE: The French fashion for arranging doors in a line (usually near the windows) so that when they are opened a long view down the length of the house can be achieved. Popular in the17th and early 18th century Baroque houses.

ENTABLATURE: The horizontal feature supported by columns (see fig 4.13).

ENTASIS: Straight-sided columns appear to curve inwards so Greeks made them slightly thicker in the middle (entasis) to counter this effect.

FLUTING: Vertical concave grooves running up a column or pilaster.

FRIEZE: The middle of the entablature (see fig 4.13).

GABLE: The triangular-shaped top of an end wall between the slopes of a roof.

GARDEROBE: The medieval word for a lavatory..

HIPPED ROOF: A roof with a slope on all four sides. A gabled roof has two vertical end walls (gables).

JAMBS: The sides of an opening for a door or window.

KEYSTONE: The top middle stone of an arch, which can be projected out as a feature.

KNOT GARDEN: A formal arrangement of patterned areas in gravel or grass and surrounded by low clipped hedges. Popular in the 16th century.

LANTERN: A small tower on top of a dome which lets light in, illuminating the interior.

LINTEL: A flat beam which is fitted above a doorway or window to take the load of the wall above.

LOGGIA: A gallery or corridor opened on one side with a row of columns.

LOUVRE: An opening, usually with slats, through which smoke can escape from a hearth.

MANSARD ROOF: A roof with a steep-sided lower section and low-pitched top part which creates more room in the attic below (named after the French architect Francois Mansard).

MOULDING: A decorative strip in wood, stone or plaster.

MULLION: A vertical bar in a window.

OCULUS: A circular opening, often on a dome or a mansard roof.

ORATORY: A small private chapel.

ORDERS: The different styles of the combined column and entablature from Classical architecture (see figs 4.13- 4.17).

ORIEL WINDOW: A large projecting window (see fig 1.5).

PALISADE: A fence comprising pales, pointed pieces of wood, and often mounted on a bank surrounding a fortified site or deer park.

PARAPET: A low wall running along the edge of the roof above the main wall, or along the top of a hipped roof on 17th century Dutch style houses.

PARTERRE: A level piece of land within a garden (from the French for 'on the ground'). A series of parterres, often in steps if the land sloped, with arrangements of flowerbeds, were popular in 17th century and early 18th century gardens.

PEDIMENT: A low-pitched triangular feature supported by columns on the top of a portico or a Classical doorway.

PENTISE: A single-pitched roof fixed to the side of a wall, which covered passages like the one which ran from the medieval hall to the kitchen.

PIANO NOBILE: The floor on which the principal rooms are contained, usually above a raised basement or ground floor.

PILASTER: A rectangular column projecting slightly from the wall, with the same treatment at the top and bottom as a freestanding column (see figs 4.13- 4.17).

PLINTH: The projecting base of a wall or the block on which a column stands (see fig 4.13).

PORTICO: A porch with a flat entablature or triangular pediment supported on columns.

QUOINS: Dressed stones at the corners of buildings.

ROTUNDA: A circular building with a dome on top (see fig 10.14).

RUSTICATION: The cutting of masonry into blocks separated by deep lines and sometimes with a rough hewn finish. Often used to distinguish the basement of Palladian houses. (see fig 4.24).

SASH: A window which slides vertically (a Yorkshire sash slides horizontally).

SCREENS PASSAGE: The space between opposing doorways at the other end of the hall from where the lord sat, which was partially closed off from the room by a wooden screen. This could be portable but was usually later fixed with two openings and a gallery above for musicians.

SHAFT: The main cylindrical part of a column (see fig 4.13).

SILL: The horizontal beam at the bottom of a window, door or timber framed wall.

SOLAR: An upper withdrawing room behind the lord's end of a medieval hall.

STATE APARTMENTS: The principal rooms within a major house, for impressing and accommodating visiting dignitaries and for ceremonial occasions.

STRING COURSE: A thin moulding which runs horizontally around a building.

STUCCO: A durable smooth plaster coating applied to the outside of houses often over brick in lieu of stone. It was particularly popular in the Regency period.

SWAG: A popular ornament in the form of a piece of fabric draped from two horizontal points, which is often found on friezes and panels especially in later 17th and 18th century decoration. A garland of fruit or flowers was sometimes used in place of the fabric though this is usually termed a festoon.

TRACERY: The ribs at the top of a stone window which are formed into patterns (usually on churches, chapels, and medieval halls).

TRANSOM: A horizontal bar in a window.

TYMPANUM: The flat triangular space within a pediment.

VAULT: An arched ceiling formed from brick or stone, and sometimes imitated in plaster and wood.

VENETIAN WINDOW: A window in three vertical sections, the centre one being taller and arched.

VOUSSOIR: A wedge-shaped stone used in the making of an arch.

WILDERNESS: Originally an area of tall clipped trees, which could be formally arranged and was popular in late 17th and early 18th garden schemes. Where they survive today, they tend to be more wild, wooded areas.

BIBLIOGRAPHY

General Books

Malcolm Airs *The Tudor and Jacobean Country House, A Building History*

Bill Breckon/Jeffrey Parker/Martin Andrew *Tracing the History of Houses*

R.W. Brunskill *Houses and Cottages of Britain*

Ingrid Cranfield *Georgian House Style*

Robin Fedden/Rosemary Joekes *The National Trust Guide*

Mark Girouard *Historic Houses of Britain*

Penny Hicks (Ed) *Historic Houses (AA Guide)*

G.E. Mingay *Land and Society in England 1750-1980*

Nigel Nicholson *The National Trust Book of Great Houses of Britain*

Nikolaus Pevsner *The Buildings of England* (most counties covered, many in conjunction with other authors)

Gervase Jackson Stops/James Pipkin *The English Country House: A Grand Tour*

Roy Strong *The Spirit of Britain*

Adrian Tinniswood *Historic Houses of the National Trust*

Margaret Wood *The English Medieval House*

Architecture Books

Mac Dowdy/Judith Miller/David Austin *Be Your Own House Detective*

John Fleming/Hugh Honour/Nikolaus Pevsner *The Penguin Dictionary of Architecture*

Hilary French *Architecture: A Crash Course*

Constance M. Grieff *Early Victorian*

Eva Howarth *A Crash Course in Architecture*

Peter Murray *The Architecture of the Italian Renaissance*

John Henry Parker *A Concise Glossary of Architectural Terms*

John Griffiths Pedley *Greek Art and Archaeology*

Leland. M. Roth *Understanding Architecture, Its Elements, History and Meaning*

David Watkin *English Architecture*

Specific Subjects

John Anthony *Discovering Period Gardens*

Gwyn Headley/Wim Meulenkamp *Follies, Grottoes and Garden Buildings*

Judith Miller *Period Kitchens*

Pamela A. Sambrook/Peter Brears (Ed) *The Country House Kitchen 1650-1900*

Alison Sim *Food and Feast in Tudor England*

Christopher Taylor *Parks and Gardens of Britain: A Landscape History from the Air*

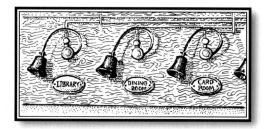

INDEX